MW01630011

Fly Tyer

LaFontaine's *Legacy*

THE LAST FLIES FROM AN AMERICAN MASTER

Al and Gretchen Beatty

THE LYONS PRESS

Guilford, Connecticut

An imprint of The Globe Pequot Press

To Gary LaFontaine

The best fly fisher and fly designer we've ever met.
Thanks, Gary, for all your help and friendship over the years.

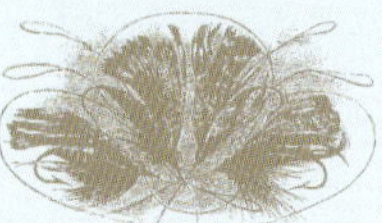

Fly Tyer, the world's leading fly-tying magazine, is proud to bring you *Fly Tyer* Books published by The Lyons Press.

Copyright © 2008 by Al Beatty and Gretchen Beatty

ALL RIGHTS RESERVED. No part of this book may be reproduced or transmitted in any form by any means, electronic or mechanical, including photocopying and recording, or by any information storage and retrieval system, except as may be expressly permitted in writing from the publisher. Requests for permission should be addressed to The Globe Pequot Press, Attn: Rights and Permissions Department, P.O. Box 480, Guilford, CT 06437.

The Lyons Press is an imprint of The Globe Pequot Press.

All interior photos by Al Beatty
Text design by Sheryl P. Kober

Library of Congress Cataloging-in-Publication Data

Beatty, Al.
  Lafontaine's legacy : the last flies from an American master / Al and Gretchen Beatty.
    p. cm.
  ISBN 978-1-59921-275-3
  1. Flies, Artificial. 2. Fly tying. I. Beatty, Gretchen. II. LaFontaine, Gary. III. Title.
  SH451.B356 2008
  688.7'9124—dc22

                                                          2008006032

Printed in China

10 9 8 7 6 5 4 3 2 1

To buy books in quantity for corporate use
or incentives, call **(800) 962–0973**
or e-mail **premiums@GlobePequot.com.**

CONTENTS

In the early 1980s, I spent much of my time fly fishing for native brook trout in the Great Smoky Mountains and Cherokee National Forest. I loved to cast bobbing dry flies onto the surface of the crystal-clear pools and catch dozens of brightly speckled trout. When I wasn't fishing, I seined the streams for insects.

The coldwater rivers and streams of western North Carolina and eastern Tennessee are some of the most productive in North America. The water was chockfull of fish; every rock teemed with mayfly and stonefly nymphs, caddis larvae, and other invertebrates. I tried tying imitations of those bugs, and many of my flies did catch fish. Then, for Christmas 1985, my wife gave me a present that revolutionized my views about fly fishing and tying: Gary LaFontaine's book *Caddisflies*. She inscribed it with the whimsical note: "I hope this book helps you build the superior caddisfly!"

In *Caddisflies*, which was first published in 1981, Gary described hundreds of the most important members of this group of insects. He gave complete descriptions of the various species, their geographic distributions, and how they lived. In many ways, Gary helped usher in the era of "bug Latin" when hardcore anglers started spewing the scientific names of insects the way the Pope speaks Latin.

A master angler, Gary took a very scientific approach to his fishing. He would collect a caddisfly, learn how it lived, tie a convincing forgery, and then discover how to fish it so that the new pattern would closely match the movement of the natural insect. He repeated this method for imitating all the important trout foods.

I think many anglers are attracted to Gary and his writings because he had achieved a sort of Zen-like oneness with trout and trout rivers. He used his knowledge of the fishes' environment and how they lived to catch and then lovingly return them to the water. Gary passed away in 2002, but fortunately for us, he left a lasting legacy through his many books, articles, and instructional tapes. And, as you will discover in this important new book, his influence continues to grow.

LaFontaine's Legacy: The Last Flies from an American Master completes the LaFontaine canon. Authors Al and Gretchen Beatty spent many hours with Gary and appeared with him at fly-fishing shows. When the ravages of Lou Gehrig's disease made it impossible for Gary to tie, he described his patterns for the audiences while his friends showed how to make the flies. In the process, Al and Gretchen received intimate knowledge of how to tie and fish Gary's last, unpublished patterns. And now, the couple shows us how to create these important flies.

Once again, Gary—with Al and Gretchen Beatty's help—has revolutionized the way I view fly fishing and tying.

—David Klausmeyer

ACKNOWLEDGMENTS

This book would have never happened without the help and friendship of Paul and Char Stimpson. They were always there when we needed encouragement, ideas, or information. We both especially thank them for their participation in the video series; it wouldn't have happened without them.

Additional thanks must go to Cathy Ransier and Marcie Chovanak, the current owners of the Book Mailer, the business started by Gary along with Stan and Glenda Bradshaw. Also, we thank Patrick and Heather (LaFontaine) Ellison for helping Gary, and us, complete the video series. We both often got a real laugh out of listening to the audiotapes of our various meetings. We both remember the day we spent with Patrick and Heather gathering video clips for the series. Heather was a real pro in front of the camera.

A special thank-you must go to Bob Lay and Jeff Smith for their encouragement during the times we wondered if we could ever finish the project. Last we must recognize Ken Magee who inspired us to get the book started; unfortunately he passed before he could see it in print. Ken, old friend, the first fish is for you!

I really get excited when we start writing another book. It's kind of how I look at the spring of a new year; it's full of wonderment, opportunity, and things yet to be discovered. Gretchen and I always start out with an outline, but somehow the book gets a mind of its own and takes its own direction. That's probably partly due to the way we write: Al assembling the original draft, followed by Gretchen taking his feeble attempts at the English language and making sense out of those words. That process often generates "discussions" that can go on for days as we mold (together of course) the raw words and photographs into a final product. Those discussions generate some really good ideas that we blend into the preliminary outline; in other words, the book takes on a character of its own as we march down the road toward the day we deliver the final manuscript to the publisher, The Lyons Press.

What really makes this book so exciting is twofold: We are working again with our good friends Paul and Char Stimpson, and the subject matter revolves around longtime friend Gary LaFontaine. As we work our way through these pages, their content will be the result of a four-way discussion, with Gary's input at almost every juncture. "Gary's input," you may ask? How can that be?

Well, that's where the story really begins. All four of us have a varied history with Gary from several different perspectives. Gretchen and I were Gary's friends who became business associates when he asked if we could produce a dubbing wax to take the place of Overton's Wonder Wax. We produced a product (BT's Super Tacky Wax) he liked, which led to our company selling his organization the wax and many other items. It was a friendship/business relationship that spanned a number of years, ending with our video company producing seven educational tapes featuring many of his patterns.

At this point, Paul and Char entered the scene. They are superb commercial fly tiers who focused much of their professional attention on LaFontaine patterns. Over the years their enthusiasm for Gary's flies eventually came to his attention at a time when amyotrophic lateral sclerosis (ALS) affected his fly-tying ability. Gary needed a pair of eyes and hands to continue doing fly-tying demonstrations, and Paul knew his flies almost as well as Gary did. The two were magic at fly-tying demonstrations; Gary narrated and told stories (lots of stories, some that were even true) while Paul tied the flies. Paul's impeccable sense of timing kept him in pace with Gary's narration—not an easy feat considering the "detours" Gary could generate with a "mostly true story." The Gary/Paul demonstrations were so similar to those Gary performed before ALS entered his life that the two seemed as one; they were definitely on the same wavelength.

So let's get back to the story of how Gary was involved in this book. Paul and I met at a show in Grand Junction, Colorado, while he was tying one of Gary's patterns, a Bead Head Marabou Worm. During the course of our conversation, we decided to shoot a video of a few of Gary's flies. After its completion we sent a copy to Gary for his approval before distributing it to the public. He really liked the video and suggested we shoot all of his flies that had never been taped before. It sounded like a good idea to us, so over the next several years we exchanged e-mails, letters, and phone calls and met multiple times to "script" each chapter in the video series, *LaFontaine Originals,* Volumes 1 through 7. We have all of those bits of correspondence among the four of us—e-mails, letters, notes from phone calls, and videotape of the scripting sessions, including many of his "mostly true stories."

Several times over the years we worked with him, Gary commented that he wanted to publish the flies developed (or improved) since his last book and had started an outline. At our last scripting session Gary asked if we could one day publish those flies for him, as he didn't think he could get the project done. I remember to this day (and we have it on tape) when Gary said, "These flies are my legacy." He then mumbled a few words and again could be heard saying something to the effect that he didn't think he had the time to get them done.

I myself wondered at times if we (Paul, Char, Gretchen, and I) could manage to bring all of our data, notes, videos, and memories to reside on these pages. It's been a tough journey, but I am pleased to bring Gary's legacy flies to print. It's taken us several years, but here we are, using all the information the four of us got from Gary, including some of his own words and thoughts when they were available.

Now you know how Gary was involved, and we have committed to portray his "legacy" as clearly as we can and as well as memory serves. However, the final results are his flies from our perspective—how they produced for us and/or information he provided in their behalf. We look forward to remembering the good times with him and sharing them with all of you. **Welcome to *LaFontaine's Legacy*!**

Al Beatty
Boise, Idaho
July 2007

Chapter 1

Antron Bi-Visible

My personal history with the Antron Bi-Visible started about five decades ago when I received my first fly-tying book as a Christmas gift, the *Professional Fly Tying and Spinning Lure Making Manual* by George Herter. (I still have that book today.) In it he referenced a couple of flies called the Trivisible and Bi-Visible.

It was a number of years before I had more than two feather colors (brown and white were all my parents had in their flock of chickens), so I was limited to the Bi-Visible fly. In time I discovered that a person could actually buy supplies—I didn't have to raid my mother's sewing basket or henhouse to obtain them. What a revelation! Along with that discovery was my second book, *Tie Your Own Flies* by Roy Patrick.

The Bi-Visible (and its three-colored cousin) became a go-to fly for my excursions to Mill Creek State Park near my early-days' home on a dairy farm just outside Sutherland, Iowa. The bluegill and crappie found it very attractive, so I used it often. The fact that I could easily get another batch of tying supplies by visiting the henhouse was another important consideration.

In time I discovered fly fishing for trout and virtually abandoned my "warmwater roots." The Bi-Visible was a pattern often snuggled away in my fly box, but it was never a favorite. It filled a need once in a while when other patterns failed. A major discovery came when I learned the pattern was supposed to be a dry fly. After many years of tying it using hen hackle (all I had at the time), causing it to sink quickly, I discovered the use of rooster hackle. Fishing the Bi-Visible on the water's surface did in fact expand my horizons. It still didn't fall into the "favorite" category, but it didn't get kicked completely out of the fly box either.

All of that changed one spring day when Gary LaFontaine called Gretchen and me to place an order. When Gary "placed an order," it was really about five minutes of business and many minutes discussing what each of us was up to in our personal lives. Family life, fishing, kids, fishing, work, fishing—I think you get the idea. We discussed our favorite subject often. On this particular call Gary talked about the book he was working on, *Fly Fishing the Mountain Lakes*. When he started to explain "blow-line fishing" to Gretchen, she stopped him and put him on the speakerphone so that we both could hear the conversation. Gary again reviewed his blow-line techniques (I took notes) and the Antron Bi-Visible he found particularly effective for this "long-line dapping method." He explained that blow-line fishing was nothing more than replacing the fly line with 90 feet of dental floss, using a float tube to get the wind to your back, and allowing the wind to blow the line/fly over the target area. When you dropped the rod tip, the pattern settled on the water; when you raised the rod tip, it flew away. Wow! What an idea!

That afternoon we headed for a small pond not far from our Montana home. We didn't have to worry about having wind. Anyone who has ever lived in Montana knows that the wind never stops blowing in that state; it just slows down a little bit from time to time. Our afternoon was one of those we often dream about, but it wasn't perfect—we didn't have any Antron for the front of our Bi-Visible flies. Two days later, after Gary's promised package arrived in the mail, we were back on the same pond, and it was an afternoon we could only dream of up to that time. The Antron made the fly easier for us to see, and something about it really proved attractive to the fish.

Since then the Antron Bi-Visible has served us well in a multitude of environments, including blow-line fishing, a technique we use often on lakes or ponds. Another discovery we've made is to tie the pattern backward. The Antron at the back of the shank covers the hook point with a shroud of lights/bubbles, effectively hiding it from some wary spring-creek trout we know about who "think they have seen it all." Boy, do they get a surprise when the Antron Bi-Visible arrives on the scene!

Gary's comments about this pattern are from information supplied by Paul Stimpson: "The Antron Bi-Visible is a pattern that I used specifically for dapping on high mountain lakes. It's a very light, all hackle fly that moves quickly as the wind catches it. But it's also a fly that works on streams just like the old style Bi-Visible. Fish it dead drift, or give it a twitch. It's super easy to see, and trout love the way it sits on its hackle tips. Use it with a black body in size #18–20 for a Trico."

Now let's tie it!

Antron Bi-Visible

Hook: Size 12 to 22, 1x long standard dry fly
Thread: Black or color of choice
Hackle: Color of choice
Front hackle: Clear Antron in a dubbing loop

Step 1.1: Mount the hook in the vise and attach the tying thread at the one-third position. Wrap to the end of the shank, and trim off any waste thread.

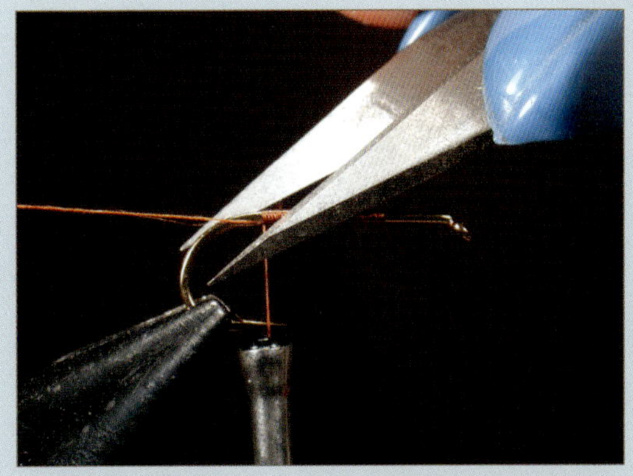

Step 1.2: Select a hackle sized to match the hook in the vise, and flare out the fibers by stroking the feather down the stem (from tip to base). Tie the feather to the hook by its tip while wrapping the thread back to the one-third position. I like to position the feather so the shiny side is forward, but this is strictly a personal call.

Step 1.3: Wrap the feather forward to meet the thread, tie it off, and trim the waste end. If you have trouble wrapping a feather that is tied in "tip first," then attach the feather to the hook at the front of the thread base, wrap to the back of the hook, and tie it off there. Trim off the waste, then palmer the thread forward through the hackle to the front of the wrapped application. Whether you elect to tie the fly front to back or back to front, it will look the same constructed either way; the choice is yours.

"

Step 1.4: Pull a long strand of thread out of the bobbin, bring it back to the hook shank, and anchor it there forming a dubbing loop. I suggest using a dubbing loop tool to assist in this part of the operation. Select a clump of clear Antron fibers, and place them in the dubbing loop. Trim them on both sides of the loop so they are similar in length.

Step 1.5: Twist the dubbing loop tool until the thread tension has spun the Antron all the way around it. Start wrapping the thread/Antron application around the hook while stroking the fibers back after each turn.

Step 1.6: Finish wrapping the Antron, tie it off, and trim away the dubbing loop. Apply a whip-finish, trim, and coat the head with cement. Use a pair of scissors to trim the Antron hackle to shape, thus finishing the fly.

Chapter 2

Bead Head Deep Sparkle Pupa

I'll never forget the first time I met Gary LaFontaine. It was in the early 1980s and we were both featured presenters at a fly-fishing show. Gary was the headliner and I was just "one of the other presenters," but somehow we ended up sitting side by side at the head table during the banquet. Quite frankly, I wasn't sure how I should speak to a "celebrity," but Gary put me right at ease when he joined me at the table, saying, "Hi, I'm Gary LaFontaine. I've been looking forward to meeting you," as he shook my hand. I was stunned he even knew who I was, but he immediately set the tone for a very relaxed, enjoyable evening. Little did I know he was setting me up for a real "jokes on me" situation that would take almost twenty years to unfold. At the time I wasn't aware of his incredibly sharp memory or crazy sense of humor.

During the course of our conversation, I shared with Gary that I really enjoyed his new book, *Caddisflies,* and the Sparkle Pupa he included along with his autograph. I further explained I was a commercial tier and was having a heck of a time learning to tie the pattern. Gary just smiled and said something to the effect, "Practice, my friend, lots of practice!" I thanked him for his "inspiration" and switched to the standard small talk anyone who has attended a few fly-fishing shows often resorts to.

A standard question involved a favorite fishing spot, and I told Gary I enjoyed the headwaters of a river located not far from his home (at that time) in Deer Lodge, Montana. He showed a lot of interest in that comment and, long story short, we eventually met to fish together on some ponds in the same general part of the state. We had a great time and caught a lot of fish on several patterns, including the Sparkle Pupa.

I returned to my home in north Idaho from that show determined to learn how to tie that darned fly. In time I got pretty good at it—in fact, I sold a few to Gary in later years for his company, the Book Mailer.

When Gretchen and I got married in the early 1990s, we moved to Bozeman, Montana, to guide and tie flies. One of the first larger commercial orders we landed was for a bunch of Deep Sparkle Pupa and its bead-headed cousin. If I remember right, the order was for a hundred, assorted dozen of each pattern.

When we started that order, Gretchen had never tied the pattern before. The Antron bubble gave her fits, and it fell to me to teach my new bride how to tie that "darned fly" (not her exact words, but close enough for this discussion). I guess we really did love each other, because our marriage survived the ordeal even after I more or less parroted Gary by saying, "Practice, my dear, practice; that's all it takes is practice!" I won't share with you her response, but you can probably guess what it may have been.

The years rolled by and we eventually moved to the Western Slope in Colorado, where I went to work for Whiting Farms as their Marketing Director. While living there we met Paul and Char Stimpson at a fly-fishing show in Grand Junction. That meeting led to a video series entitled *LaFontaine Originals,* Volumes 1 through 7. I guess this book is really a product of that meeting, but a lot of water had to pass under the bridge before it even seemed a possibility.

Scripting the video series with Gary was a very special time for all of us. On a number of occasions we (Paul, Char, Gretchen, and I) traveled to Montana to decide what should be on the next video and the message Gary wanted us to bring forth regarding each pattern. The scripting sessions followed a loose but very formal process: (1) Select the pattern and decide where in the video it would appear; (2) write down any of the comments Gary wanted presented during the taping process; and (3) tie the fly with the camera focused on the vise while Gary and Paul (or the person tying the fly) were on remote microphones. At the end of a session we would walk away with written notes and a videotaped fly with Gary's and the tier's comments. Later the four of us would meet to capture the footage we needed to edit a completed tape; we used the information/recorded comments to help put together the final product.

At one of the scripting sessions, the Bead Head Sparkle Pupa was the topic of discussion. Gary asked that we use his daughter Heather to tie the pattern when we filmed it. We agreed, but I had to ask why. He responded, "I never could tie that fly worth a darn [language cleaned up here], that's why I always had Heather tie it for me!" I looked at him in stunned silence. He started to laugh and went on to explain to everyone in the room how he had told me years earlier at a show that if I practiced the fly a lot, I could learn how to tie it.

Yes, my friends, Gary got me that day. It wasn't the first time his sense of humor or incredible memory made one of us the topic of a joke, but I'll remember that one for a long time. So now I turn this fly over to those of you reading this book—and don't complain if you have trouble tying it. I'll say to you like Gary said to me, "Practice, my friend, lots of practice!"

Here are Gary's comments about fishing the fly from *LaFontaine Originals*, Volume 6: "The reason we [the Book Mailer] had to tie the bead-head variation was the bead-head craze hit the country after the publication of *Caddisflies* in 1981. We still tie the nonbead version, and I like to fish those patterns dead drift. But I'll fish the bead-head variation when fishing a swinging fly. I love the way it cuts through the water. I mend, mend, mend to hold it in the current as long as I can."

Bead Head Sparkle Pupa

Hook: Size 8 to 16, 1x long nymph or dry fly

Thread: Color to match the insect or black

Bubble: Antron yarn, combed

Underbody: Antron touch dubbing, color to match the insect

Legs: Soft hackle fibers (optional)

Collar: Dubbing, color of choice (I used hare's ear)

Head: Brass bead (gold or color of choice)

Step 2.1: Slip the bead on the hook, and mount it in the vise. Attach the tying thread just behind the bead, and wrap to the center of the shank. Clip off the waste end of the thread.

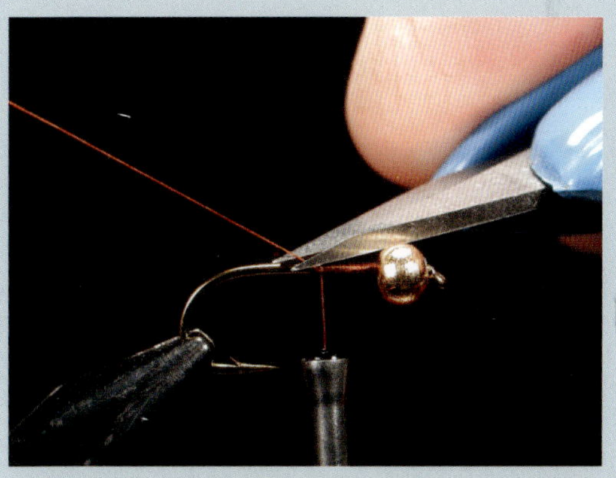

Step 2.2: Select a section of Antron yarn, and separate it into segments. Comb two of them out to separate the fibers. Tie one on the top and the other on the bottom of the hook, using one turn in the center of the shank. The one turn allows you to move the fibers around under the thread until they are evenly distributed around the shank. Wrap the thread to the back of the shank to anchor the Antron in place. Keep the application sparse, per Gary's instructions. Remove a few fibers if the Antron seems to be "overdressed."

Step 2.3: Apply dubbing to the thread and wrap it forward, forming the underbody. Here I've used clear Antron and a dark dubbed body for illustration purposes. You may find the actual insect in your part of the world has a darker "bubble" with a lighter body, like many of the caddis do here in Idaho. Study the nymphs and the adults in your waters to develop your own color combinations.

Step 2.4: Pull the Antron fibers over the brown dubbing, and tie them in front of the body. I find that if you pull the fibers forward tight, hold them in place with a couple of snug (not tight) thread wraps, and use a bodkin or scissor point to "pull out" the fibers, the bubble is a lot easier to form.

Step 2.5: After the bubble is formed, apply several very tight thread turns to anchor the Antron. Trim away the excess fibers. (I find using several snips going around the hook easier than trying to cut all of them at once.) If you plan on adding soft-hackle legs, now is the time to do so. I added a couple of turns of feather from a brown hen cape, but any good soft hackle will work just fine.

Step 2.6: Add dubbing to the thread (color of choice to match the natural), and wrap a collar between the hackle and the bead. Complete the fly with a whip-finish.

Chapter 3

Bead Head Marabou Worm

*T*his fly was really the start of the pages you see here, but at the time Paul and I first discussed it, we had no idea where destiny would lead us. We were just two people who have the same loose screw—we love to tie flies and talk about it.

I can't believe how many years have come and gone since we first met at a fly-fishing show in Grand Junction, Colorado, in early 2000. Gretchen and I had known that Paul and Char Stimpson were fellow members of the Federation of Fly Fishers but had never gotten to know them very well. When I finished my assigned time at the demonstration table and Gretchen was taking my place, she suggested I look up Paul. She thought he was tying some interesting flies that we might want to use for a magazine article. I helped set up her demonstration equipment, put mine in the car, and wandered the show looking for new ideas, all the time keeping an eye out for Paul.

In time I found where he was demonstrating, and when his audience moved on to observe another tier, I slipped into the chair across from him. Paul explained that he was tying Gary LaFontaine's Miracle Fly (the Bead Head Marabou Worm) and provided in-depth detail into its construction. The fly, and Paul's superb demonstration, really piqued my interest. We decided to shoot a video featuring this fly and several other patterns Gary had never before captured on tape. We sat together during that evening's banquet to put together a plan, deciding the general outline of a script of LaFontaine patterns we could easily produce during a three-day shoot. We were excited about the possibilities of working together on the production.

Later that spring Paul and Char visited us at our home in Delta, Colorado, where we spent several days gathering the video clips needed to produce the first tape. It was interesting to sit together in the morning over a cup of coffee before going to work and discuss our different perspectives on Gary. At the end of three days, a mutual respect for one another's ability had grown into a strong friendship—a friendship also influenced by Gary; we just weren't aware how much he would affect us over the next years.

Several weeks later I finished editing the raw footage into a master tape, made several copies, and sent one to Paul and Char to review. A couple of days later they telephoned advising that the final version "looked good" and suggested it was time to send the tape to Gary for his approval.

I must admit I sent the video to Gary with more than a little trepidation; to me he was (and would always be) the "celebrity" I had met years earlier. Even after all the business that had transpired between us, I guess I was still a bit in awe of him; it's a feeling that never did go away.

I sent the tape to Gary with a note asking him to approve it for release to the public and left on a business trip for my job at Whiting Farms. When I returned there was a message on my answering machine from Gary telling me, "Al, call as soon as you can!" The first thought to bounce into my mind, "He didn't like the tape." I made the call, holding my breath as I waited for Gary to answer the phone. All my concerns melted away when he told how much he liked the video. Then he explained that he wanted us to capture *all* his new and never-before-taped flies in a whole series of videos. It was a project that would keep the five of us quite busy for the next couple years and eventually led to the pages you see here today.

Comments from *LaFontaine Originals,* Volume 1, and associated notes: The pattern entered this world as the Marabou Worm in Gary's book *Trout Flies Proven Patterns.* As the years passed, Gary's friends reported that a bead head added to the fly really improved their angling success. Ever wondering why, Gary asked a dive team to find out. They observed that the beaded fly tumbled in the current like the original pattern, but the bead also provided a bit of flash that seemed to focus the fish's attention to the action.

Something I learned from Gary is that earthworms can remain alive for extended periods underwater, so they mix well with the aquatic worms sharing that environment. Often both varieties are available to the resident fish after a rainstorm—one gets washed in from the surrounding earth, while the increased water flow can disturb the aquatic variety. Now I understand why this pattern is so successful for me when the water is a bit off color. I always thought the flash of the bead head was the reason the pattern fished so much better in off-color water, but while that could be an important consideration, Gary thought their larger numbers of worms in the water after a rainstorm was at least a factor, if not the main reason. I certainly won't argue with his premise; I just know I catch a heck of a lot of fish with them (both warm- and coldwater species) when the water is off color after a rain.

The fly must look like a really good meal, because I seem to catch larger fish on it—or at least I kid myself into thinking I do. In *Trout Flies Proven Patterns,* Gary he has the same thought: "Here is a fact on the Marabou Worm—I have fished it on an average of three days a season over the past nine years, and yet in five of those years it caught the biggest trout. Obviously, it isn't a random fly for me."

It's not for me either, maintaining an important position in my personal fly box. It should be in yours as well.

Bead Head Marabou Worm

Hook: Size 8 to 18, 2x long nymph hook

Thread: Color to match marabou

Bead: Gold bead, sized to match the hook

Tail float: Edgewater foam cylinder

Tail and body: Marabou—olive, gray, red, or black

Step 3.1: Slip a bead on the hook, mount it in the vise, attach the thread, and wrap to the end of the shank. Trim off the waste end. Cut a short section of a foam cylinder, and use a bodkin to place a hole through the center. Set it aside to allow the bodkin to "stretch" the hole for a minute; it makes inserting the marabou in the next step much easier.

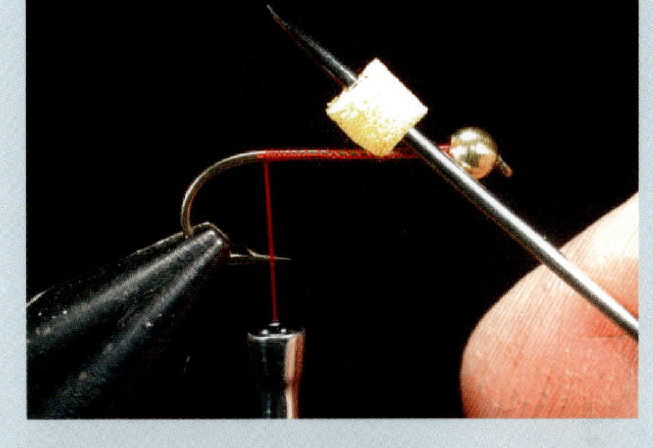

Step 3.2: Strip the marabou fibers from the base of the stem. Remove the bodkin from the foam cylinder, and insert the stripped part of the stem through the hole left by the tool. Slide the foam cylinder toward the end of the feather, stopping about a shank length short of the fiber tips.

Step 3.3: Tie the feather on the hook at the end of the shank, forming a tail that is twice the hook in length.

Step 3.4: Twist the feather *and* the thread together in preparation to wrap the body in the next step.

Step 3.5: Wrap the body forward to meet the bead. Tie it off, and trim away the waste part of the feather.

Step 3.6: Whip-finish the thread, trim it from the hook, and place a drop of cement on the head. Finish the fly by placing a bit of superglue next to the foam cylinder; allow the glue to soak down into the hole, anchoring the foam in place.

Chapter 4

Bead Head Peacock Twist Nymph

I first heard the term "Double Magic" when Paul Stimpson referenced it at a fly-fishing show Gretchen and I helped organize in Grand Junction, Colorado. We were on the show committee as well as doing tying demonstrations when time allowed. After several hours at the vise, I needed to give my voice a break and decided to wander the show. So where does a fly tier go when he needs a break? To watch other fly tiers, of course! And that's just what I did.

After a quick tour through the fly-tying area, I had spotted several demonstrators I wanted to spend additional time with, including Paul. Gretchen had suggested I check out his patterns, and after observing his presentation, I could certainly see why she found them interesting. He explained the steps in detail without seeming to talk down to the audience, and he tied flies like the commercial tier he was—practiced, smooth, and self-assured. I've always prided myself on being able to spot a commercial tier in a heartbeat, and Paul's skills were evident from clear across the room.

When the audience moved on from his tying station, I slipped into the chair across from Paul and introduced myself. He explained he was tying some LaFontaine patterns, like the Bead Head Marabou Worm and another utilizing a technique he called "Double Magic." He explained that Gary had coined the phrase in reference to the magical properties of peacock herl and Antron in his book *Trout Flies Proven Patterns.* Gary later used the term extensively in his many tying demonstrations and an appearance on a Jack Dennis video production.

When Paul showed me how to apply Double Magic to a hook, I thought to myself, *You got to be kidding me!* I really didn't think a mixture of two materials I had long held in high regard could actually have as much impact on fish as Paul implied, but still, you never know. It was one of those bits of information often gleaned at a show that certainly deserved additional investigation.

After returning home—and a short trip to my library to verify Gary's thoughts in his book—I took my skepticism about the Double Magic technique to my fly-tying vise. The process was easy enough to duplicate, but the question kept banging around in my head: *Would it work on the fish near my Colorado home?* Determined to find out, I tied several of the bead-headed version of Gary's Twist Nymph that Paul had demonstrated at the show.

I took a half dozen of the flies and my fishing equipment to work the next day. On the way home that evening, I stopped at a group of ponds that held large, selective trout. Those fish hadn't gotten large by being stupid and quite frankly had often given me a whipping. To say they were less than easy to catch was a gross understatement. I tied on a small Double Magic fly, made a cast, and a nearby fish actually took a look at it. That was a heck of a lot better than being ignored—my normal result. Three casts later I made my first hookup of the evening. I was so surprised, I broke the tippet from setting the hook too hard. Wow! Now I was excited.

I only had a spare hour to spend before heading for home, but during that time I hooked three more fish, landing the smallest, a brown trout near 20 inches. That evening I went from being a skeptic to a believer, big time!

Today the Double Magic technique has crept into many of my personal fly patterns. I really think it has been the most important innovation in my personal fly-fishing in the past ten years. Can it be overdone? I'm sure it can. So far, though, I've not found a situation where I didn't feel it made a real difference in my angling results.

If all of you reading these pages learn one thing, and only one thing, it should be the awesome power of the LaFontaine Double Magic technique. Now join me in tying the first of several Double Magic flies. I'll bet you will find some of your own patterns much improved when you use *the* "Magic Touch."

Bead Head Peacock Twist Nymph

Hook: Size 10 to 20, 2x long nymph

Thread: Color to match body accent

Bead: Gold, color of choice

Tail: Marabou, color of choice

Body: Peacock herl, sparse

Body accent: Antron touch dubbing, orange or color of choice

Collar: Olive touch dubbing

Step 4.1: Slip a bead on the hook, and place it in the vise. Attach the tying thread tight behind the bead; wrap to the end of the shank and back to the starting point. Trim the waste part of the thread at the back of the hook.

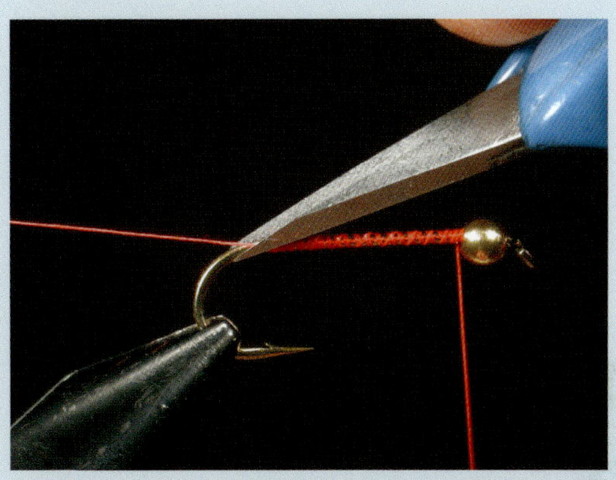

Step 4.2: Select a sparse clump of marabou, and bind it to the hook to form a tail that is a bit shorter than the hook shank. Trim the waste tight behind the bead.

Step 4.3: Select a few peacock herls, and tie them to the back of the hook by their tips. On the larger illustrated pattern, I needed several peacock herls, but when tying a smaller "fishing" fly, one or two is plenty.

Step 4.4: Apply dubbing wax (I used BT's Super Tacky) to the thread, then "touch" the dubbing to the sticky thread. *Do not* twist the dubbing into a "noodle" on the thread like most fly tiers would. Instead leave it sticking out around the thread, held in place by the dubbing wax.

Step 4.5: Place the peacock herl next to the thread, form a dubbing loop, and anchor it with a tool. (I like to use EZY hackle pliers, but any similar tool will do.) Wrap the thread forward to a position behind the bead. Twist the tool/dubbing/herl into peacock chenille with highlights of Antron. Wrap this forward to meet the thread. In the illustration I have wrapped the "assembly" forward almost to the end of the body. Be sure to leave ample room for a dubbed collar in the next step.

Step 4.6: Finish wrapping the body, tie off the chenille, and trim the waste end. Apply another coat of dubbing wax, followed with olive touch dubbing. Again, *do not* twist the dubbing around the thread. Instead wrap it to form a collar, apply a whip-finish, and trim the thread from the hook. Apply a drop of head cement to complete the fly.

Chapter 5

Diving Blue-Winged Olive Egg Layer

*L*ife is full of revelations. Some are "heart stopping," others fall in the "light-bulb on" category, and the bulk of them fall in the "interesting, nice to know" area. They run the gamut from what it's like for a father to hold his newborn child to experiences like finally understanding how to tie a blood knot that will stay together after struggling with its construction for years. The two aforementioned items are certainly in different categories of importance, but they're both part of the overall experience we call *life*. I mark one under the heading **Family** and the other under a general topic, **Fly fishing**.

Since my focus here is fly fishing and tying, I'll temporarily set aside some of the more important items in favor of that. Within that category I have a whole list of subcategories that have proven valuable to my overall skill level—things that really changed how I approach the fish, water, and tying.

Let's set aside the normal evolution any fly fisher goes through in reaching a skill set that equals the title "experienced" or some similar word. We all go through that process if we truly want to improve our skills. Let me focus instead on the revelations that are a major part of that evolutionary process. I think my first such experience was on the Clark Fork River in western Montana at least twenty-five years ago. After several fishless hours, I asked my on-stream partner at the time, Ray Miles, if he had any ideas on what we could do to break our run of bad luck. His solution was the same one he always resorted to—constantly moving along the river, hoping to locate "working" (stupid) fish. It always worked for him. Often Ray would cover a half mile of riverbank looking for working fishing, while I would cover only a couple hundred yards searching for *the* answer. Often Ray's method worked well; other times, mine brought success. Neither system was working that day.

As I sat on the riverbank puffing on a cigar and wondering what to do, I saw a good-size gray, adult caddisfly dive straight into the water and start swimming into the depths. I had never observed this type of activity before, but the one thing I did notice was that this caddis only swam a short distance before it disappeared in a subsurface flash. During the next ten minutes I saw the same thing happen several more times, but it was far enough away in each instance that I could not see if the caddis made it to the bottom to deposit its eggs or not.

The idea lightbulb flashed on over my head. I immediately dug through my fly box, where I found a #12 Iron Blue traditional wet fly. I tied it to my tippet along with a bit of twist-on lead, made a cast along with a couple of stack mends, and was soon into a jumping rainbow trout. Several fish later, my ole buddy Ray was tapping me on the shoulder, wanting to know what I was doing different—and asking if I would loan (give) him several flies.

I don't remember much more about the day—too many years have come and gone—but I will never forget that caddis diving straight into the water. I guess that scene will be burned into my memory banks forever. Other similar events have come and gone over the years, and my purpose here is not to bore all of you with them. Well, maybe just one more!

We were working on the script to one of the videos when Gary proclaimed out of the blue that male blue-winged olives accompanied the females on their trip to deposit eggs in the water's depths. The males helped provide a diversion for the females, sacrificing themselves to give the species a better chance at survival. This bit of information left me stunned. I didn't know the BWO female swam to the bottom of the water to lay its eggs, and I certainly wasn't aware the males accompanied them.

It started to make sense when Gary asked us, "Have you ever seen a BWO spinner fall?" I must have rotated his question over in my mind for the better part of ten minutes and finally had to acknowledge that I could not remember ever seeing a BWO spinner fall. Gary chuckled when we all nodded in agreement. He went on to explain the BWO phenomenon he and the dive team had observed over the years. His goal at the time was to write a book on the life cycle of the blue-winged olive similar in scope to his magnificent work *Caddisflies,* published in 1981. Unfortunately his passing brought an end to that objective. Gary's computer was checked thoroughly after his passing, but no one could find enough information to develop an outline.

The fly you see here today is all we have left of Gary's observations of the life cycle of the BWO. It's a very simple wet fly designed to mimic the adults' activity as Gary observed it. I'm sure there are skilled entomologists who can provide insight into this mayfly's habits and whether his observations are correct. I will just take what Gary offers on the belief that he is right. Besides, I catch one heck of a lot of fish on this pattern, so I won't argue with success!

Diving Blue-Winged Olive Egg Layer

Hook: Size 14 to 22, 1x long wet-style

Thread: Olive

Weight: Lead wire under the thorax

Tail: Dun hackle fibers

Body: Olive dubbing

Wing: Clear Antron

Hackle: Dun hackle fibers, beard style

Head: Olive dubbing

Step 5.1: Place the hook in the vise, and mentally divide the shank into four equal parts. Start the tying thread at the one-fourth position back from the eye, then wrap to the end of the shank. Select a clump of dun hackle fibers, and tie them to the hook to form a tail equal in length to the shank. Wrap to the front of the thread base, and trim the waste tail fibers.

Step 5.2: Select a section of lead wire, and attach it to the bottom of the hook shank. Wrap back to the center of the hook, binding the wire in place. Pull the excess portion of the wire down and slightly back, then trim it with the scissors parallel with the hook shank. Trimming the wire at this angle provides a smooth taper, thus forming part of the underbody. Wrap over the trimmed end, then apply a bit of head cement to keep the lead wire from later staining the body when the fly gets wet.

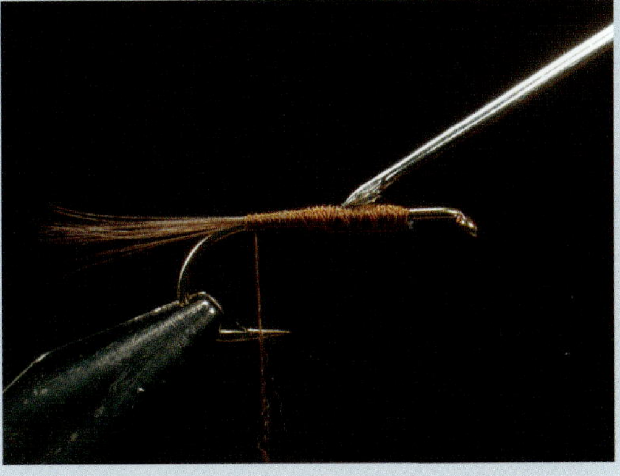

Step 5.3: Apply dubbing to the thread (using the standard twist method), and wrap the body, stopping at the front of the hook. Be certain to leave room for the hackle, wing, and head. At this point you have some interesting options for this fly (or other patterns). You could add a rib of thread, wire, or tinsel. How about a thread rib with a bit of touch dubbing attached to it but not twisted into a noodle Double Magic style? Think about it! The possibilities could be interesting; just let your imagination run wild. Gary would like that!

Step 5.4: Select a 6-inch piece of Antron yarn, divide it in half, and tie it to the hook centered in the middle of the strand. Fold over the forward-facing part of the strand, and tie it in position to form the wing.

Step 5.5: Apply several thread wraps to cover the fold-over point, then use a pair of scissors to cut the wing to length. Gary suggested trimming it even with the end of the body. Use a fine-tooth comb to separate the fibers. The pictured comb is available through the Book Mailer (www.thebookmailer.com), the company Gary and Stan Bradshaw started. I think it is worth every cent.

Step 5.6: Select several strands of dun hackle fibers, and tie them to the bottom of the hook to form a beard-style application. Trim off the waste fibers, taking care to not clip the thread in the process.

Step 5.7: Apply dubbing to the thread, and construct the pattern's head. Again, this would be a fun place to use touch dubbing, as illustrated on the pattern's head in the previous chapter.

Step 5.8: Complete the tying process by using a whip-finish tool to wrap the thread part of the head. A coating of cement will finish the fly.

Chapter 6

Diving Egg–Laying Midge

*A*s I turned off the state highway onto a county road leading into a desert canyon, the temperature readout inside my truck told me it was a heck of a lot hotter outside than it was inside the air-conditioned cab. My canine companion and fishing dog, Dubbin, grew restless, either from anticipation of reaching our destination or the scorching heat waiting for us.

Several miles later I could see the white pickup dwarfed by the canyon walls that signaled the end of our trip. Waiting there were friends Jeff Smith and his son Steve. The heat hit me hard in the face as I stepped out of the truck to ask the standard fly-fishing question, "Hey guys. Anything happening?" Of course my comment could have covered a range of topics, but we all knew it referenced the tailwater fishery that lay before us. "It's kind of quiet," responded Jeff as Dubbin ran down the bank and plopped himself in the water to stay cool.

We discussed "hatches" and whether we thought they might "come off today." We anticipated a fairly good midge hatch in an hour or so as the late afternoon blended into the longer shadows of evening, bringing us to the "magic hour"—or so we hoped. Jeff had made a bug seine that morning out of a section of screen and two old broom handles. "Let's see what's in the drift," he suggested. It sounded like a good idea, but one that required a major decision. Do we put on our waders or wade wet? Jeff and I opted to slip into our waders, while Steve indicated he was just going into the cold water in his sneakers and shorts. As much as I didn't want to slip on my waders in the hot afternoon sun, I knew that as soon as the sun left the canyon, the desert air would drop several degrees, making me glad I had braved the heat earlier in the day. A little over an hour later, I was darned glad to have on my waders.

For now, stepping into the cold water coming out of the dam made wearing the waders much more bearable to see what was "in the drift." All three of us were stunned to see how many critters collected in the screen in a very short time. It was the first time we had seined this section of the river, and the biomass was almost overwhelming. There were a few mayfly nymphs and millions of midge larvae in a range of colors and sizes. In some parts of the screen, we couldn't see the seine because the volume of bugs completely covered it.

I didn't have any doubt what pattern I was going to try. The day before I had rediscovered a several-year-old e-mail from Gary explaining about his Diving Egg-Laying Midge pattern and how effective it was when he fished it in late fall in some of his Montana waters. Gary's e-mail had described several scuba-diving excursions where he discovered adult midges crawling underwater on the edges of the ice. He observed the trout cruising the edges of the ice and turning those midges into the main course for their dinner.

To quote a portion of his e-mail: "I'll fish this fly dead drift in rivers. In lakes I'll often string two or three flies on a leader, let my cast sink, and then draw the flies slowly toward the top."

As we were studying the seine full of bugs, I didn't know if Gary's suggestions would translate into success on this desert tailwater fishery or not, but I knew I had to give them a good try.

Not long after we put away the seine and rigged up our fly rods, the sun dipped below the canyon wall, the shadows grew long, and the river came alive with feeding fish everywhere. *Will a fly with an Antron wing fool any of these fish when so many naturals are available in the water?* was a question that kept banging around in my head. I didn't have long to wait for the answer.

I had only dead-drifted my tiny brown offering less than a dozen presentations when my tippet made a subtle twitch and I set the hook. I was fast into a really strong fish that shot across the river before I could slow it down. Eventually I led it back to my side of the river and got it close enough to see that it was a really large brown trout, well over 20 inches. I finally slid the tired fish next to my feet, measured it in the water by comparing it to my fly rod, and used my Ketchum Release tool to set it free. I got out my tape measure and compared it to the point on my fly rod that approximated the length of the fish. I don't have an exact measurement, but the fish was at least 22 inches long—the biggest river fish I had caught on a fly smaller than a #20 in several years. I mentally thanked Gary for a memorable moment, then went back to fishing. The evening unfolded into a great adventure with several more "fun-size" fish to hand until the cold water and evening air drove me to the bank to get warm. I decided to call it a day and wandered back to my truck, where I met Jeff and Steve also packing up for their trip home.

They had enjoyed a super evening, with several "good" fish to their credit. We chatted for a few minutes, and then Dubbin and I headed for home. It dawned on me that my fishing dog had not left my side the whole day. Usually when I fish with Jeff, Dubbin spends most of his time with him rather than me. Why? Because Jeff usually catches more fish than I do, and Dubbin is always where "the action" is. That day, I guess, the action was with me. I smiled and quietly thanked Gary for a fun evening, sensing his presence as I drove out of the canyon, back into the real world, and home to share the experience with Gretchen.

Diving Egg-Laying Midge

Hook: Size 16 to 22, 1x long, wet-style

Thread: Brown

Body: Brown touch dubbing, sparse

Wing: Clear Antron, looped

Hackle: Brown, one turn

Color options: hackle to match body: Black, olive, red, brown, gray, cream, and clear (white hackle with the clear)

Step 6.1: Mount the hook in the vise, and attach the thread two eye-widths back on the shank. Wrap to the end of the hook and slightly down into the bend. Trim the excess part of the thread.

Step 6.2: Swipe the thread a couple of times with a good, tacky wax, making certain to evenly distribute it along the strand. Pat the thread with brown touch dubbing, keeping the application fairly sparse. *Do not* twist the dubbing into a noodle. Our goal is a thread body with Antron highlights, not a heavily dubbed body. Start wrapping the highlighted thread forward.

Step 6.3: Finish wrapping the last part of the body. If you have more touch dubbing than needed, it can be easily removed. Select a strand of Antron yarn, and fold it in half to make a looped wing. Tie on the wing flat so that it is long enough to reach a position even with the hook barb. Gretchen and I find folding the Antron over a bodkin helpful in keeping the wing profile nice and neat. Keep the wing sparse; I used half the fibers I thought it needed, and it is still fuller than Gary would have preferred.

Step 6.4: Trim off the waste fibers from the wing, and set them aside for use on a future fly. Select a brown hackle feather, and strip the fuzzy fibers from the base of the stem. Tie it to the hook with the shiny side facing forward. Grasp the feather with hackle pliers in preparation for the next step.

Step 6.5: Wrap the hackle around the hook once, and tie it off. Trim the excess part of the feather. Set it aside for use on another fly if sufficient material remains.

Step 6.6: Wrap a thread head, then apply a whip-finish. Complete the fly by trimming the thread and placing head cement over the whip-finish.

Drop Nose Minnow

ntil the four of us spent time with Gary filming his flies and learning his thought process behind each pattern, I must admit I was fairly "ho-hum" about the importance of eyes on a fly. Yes, I had read all of Gary's books, but quite frankly there is something very different about reading what a person thinks and talking with them in person about the same subject; at least it is for me.

There was something about the light in his eyes that made me really sit up and take notice when we were discussing this crazy-looking pattern before we filmed it. We discussed "strike zones" (something new to me at that time), as I remember the conversation. As I quizzed him about the pattern, he filled in the details. Gary emphasized the eyes on this pattern because he felt a predatory fish would strike at that location on the fly. He placed the eyes at the back of the hook because that placed the strike zone directly adjacent to the business end of the hook. Gary believed he encountered fewer "short strikes" and therefore lost fewer fish with the eyes positioned at the back of the hook. I didn't disbelieve him, but still wasn't convinced.

I asked about other parts of the fly and their purpose. The double bead in the front was to give the fly a "jigging action" during the retrieve. The calf tail under-wing provided support for the marabou overwing so that it was less prone to tangle around the hook. And the rest of the fly used materials in its construction that often proved successful on other streamer patterns. Yes, I certainly could support those theories; they just plain made sense.

I still was not convinced about the eyes, and I guess my hesitation was evident. Gary finally said something like, "So, you're not a believer?" I had to admit I was struggling with the concept. I considered myself a better-than-average streamer fisherman, having learned the techniques from a couple of the best fly fishers I knew. They hadn't considered eyes important on their streamers, and therefore I didn't either. I told Gary as much, and he just kind of grinned. He offered a couple of bits of anecdotal evidence to support his theory, in the process extracting a promise from me to at least try a few streamers with eyes in their construction.

We continued the job at hand, which was scripting another of the *LaFontaine*

Originals video segments. At the end of the day Gary again reminded me to give eyes on my streamers a try. I promised I would and headed for home.

Gretchen and I had a long drive in front of us, and we spent a good portion of it discussing the events of past day with Gary. Of course my promise to try streamers with eyes slipped into the conversation, and Gretchen just kind of grinned as we discussed the pros and cons of his theories. When we got back to our home (at that time in western Colorado), she told me she had a surprise for me. She reached into her suitcase and pulled out the Drop Nose Minnow that Paul had tied during our scripting session with Gary. I thought he had ended up with it, but obviously I was wrong. I was going to give his theory a test drive quicker than I had anticipated.

The next evening after work, we headed to a favorite stretch of the Gunnison River upstream from our home. Without giving away any favorite locations, we ended up at the river after a long, tough drive on a four-wheel-drive section of road. When we arrived at the river, we rigged up our fly rods, all the time keeping an eye on the weather. When we left home it was bright and sunny, but a bank of clouds rolling in from the west threatened to dump rain all over our test drive of the Drop Nose Minnow.

Anyone who has lived in western Colorado soon learns how slick a rain can make the dirt roads; they are some of the most treacherous we've ever encountered. Caution prevailed over the want to test the fly, and we left for home only a few minutes after arriving at the river. It turns out it was a good decision—the sky opened up and the rain was pouring like crazy about a half mile before we got back to a gravel road. That last half mile was a bit scary, to say the least, but we were thankful we were not back at the river with 10 miles of bad road before us. Oh, well, the best laid plans, etc., etc.

The next morning we took our dog, Dubbin, for a walk at a lake not far from the house. As we got back to the truck from the walk, I could see a school of fish cruising the shallows a few feet from the bank. What the heck! The rod was still rigged up from the previous evening, so I punched a cast toward the pod of fish. I let the fly sink for several seconds, gave it two strips, and let it settle a bit longer. About halfway through the second retrieve, I connected with a fish that ran my line about 30 feet then stopped to shake its head.

About ten minutes later I landed a 2-foot-long carp. I had been trying to catch one of those fish for several weeks. I was excited about that, but I also had a dilemma. How in the heck could I tell someone with Gary LaFontaine's stature in the fly-fishing community that my first fish on his pattern was a carp! Oh, the shame of it! I took the coward's way out and never told him. I can almost feel him now, looking over my shoulder as I type these words laughing his ...ah, well, you know...off!

As funny as is may seem, that carp convinced me I should give Gary's theories consideration. After several years, many different waters, and a lot of experimentation, a major portion of my subsurface flies now have eyes on them. Need I say more? Let's tie this fly before I give up some more embarrassing moments to all of you!

Drop Nose Minnow

Hook: Size 2 to 10, 3x long streamer

Thread: Black, white, red

Beads: Large silver behind small black

Tail: Silver Krystal Flash

Eyes: Doll, stick-on or painted, at the end of the shank

Rear body: Orange touch dubbing, four strands Krystal Flash

Front body: White Antron yarn

Underwing: White calf tail

Wing: White marabou

Overwing: Green Krystal Flash

Gills/throat: Red yarn, combed

Gray materials were used in the illustrations rather than white as suggested in the recipe to help provide photographic clarity.

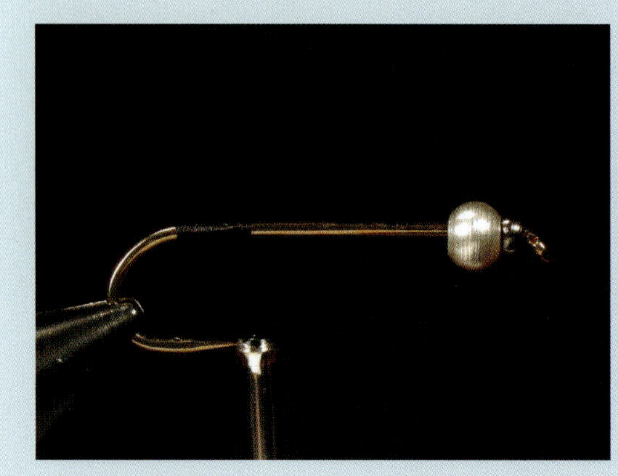

Step 7.1: Slip a small black and a large silver bead on the hook, then mount it in the vise. Attach black tying thread at the back of the hook shank, and trim off the waste end.

Step 7.2: Select a clump of silver Krystal Flash, and tie it to the shank pointing to the rear of the hook. Trim the Krystal Flash to form a tail equal to the hook gape in length.

Step 7.3: Wrap a large thread base at the back of the shank on which to place the eyes, then whip-finish and trim it from the hook. I am using stick-on eyes, but paint could be used as well. Apply a couple of coats of glue to cover the thread base and the eyes. Allow each coat to dry before applying the next.

Step 7.4: Attach white tying thread in front of the eye assembly, then trim the tag end. Select several strands of silver Krystal Flash, and tie them to the hook. Apply dubbing wax to the thread, then "pat" orange touch dubbing to it. Form the thread into a dubbing loop, and capture the Krystal Flash in it using a tool. Twist the tool/loop to form a Krystal Flash application with orange Antron highlights Double Magic style, as described in chapter 4 on the Peacock Twist Nymph. Wrap the Double Magic assembly over the back part of the hook to form that part of the body.

Step 7.5: Finish wrapping the back part of the body, tie it off, and trim the waste. Select a segment of white Antron yarn, and tie it to the front part of the hook (behind the beads). Wrap it forward almost all the way to the beads, tie it off, and trim away the excess. Be sure to leave room for the wing and the collar/throat assemblies.

Step 7.6: Clip a tuft of calf tail fibers, clean out the underfur, and place them in a hair stacker with the tips pointing down. Even the fibers, and tie them to the hook to form an underwing long enough to reach the end of the tail. Trim off the waste ends.

Step 7.7: Select a white marabou feather, and strip the shorter fibers from the base of the stem. Tie it to the hook as an overwing equal in length to the calf tail placed in the last step.

Step 7.8: Cut a section of green Krystal Flash from the bundle, and tie it to the hook as a wing topping. Trim the Krystal Flash so that the fibers are even with the rest of the wing assembly. Whip-finish the white thread, and attached the red. Trim as needed.

Step 7.9: Separate one segment from a four-strand piece of red yarn, and tie it to the hook between the wing and beads. Wrap about three turns of the material, and tie it off. Pull the excess yarn down and back, then wrap several thread turns to force them to stay in that position. Whip-finish the thread.

Step 7.10: Trim the thread from the hook, and cut the waste end of the yarn long to form the throat. I pulled it tight and cut it even with the end of the front part of the body. Use a fine-tooth comb (available from the Book Mailer) to fuzz out the throat fibers. I like rotating the vise a half turn to accomplish this task, but it can easily be done without moving the fly; it's your choice.

Chapter 8

Drowned Trico

*T*urning off Interstate 90 south toward Hardin, Montana, the "tick-tock" of the turn signal seemed to be in tune with the "slip-slap" sound of the windshield wipers keeping time with Willie's "On the Road Again" coming from the radio. Wow! Either this was a major coincidence or I was more exhausted than I thought. The mind can really play tricks, and mine was working overtime.

It was two o'clock in the morning. I could look back eight hours to getting off work in midafternoon and heading for Fort Smith, Montana, and the Bighorn River. Along the way I picked up my fishing partner, Bob Lay, who had long since fallen asleep in the seat beside me. I was rolling over in my mind, *Am I sane or not, putting myself through this "fun" just to go fishing,* but something about the call of the next week on the river during the fall black caddis hatch seemed to quiet my concerns. Then Bob started snoring, and I no longer needed the "noise" of the radio to keep me awake.

As I slowed down to traverse the sharp left turn in the road at St. Xavier, Bob jerked awake and wanted to know, "Are we there yet?" I responded, "Another fifteen minutes, you might as well wake up and get ready to unpack."

He commented about the thick fog, and I told him we had run into it several miles back. A few minutes later we pulled into the trailer park behind the restaurant and started driving up and down the streets looking for our rented trailer and home for the next week. We found it, moved in, and I was asleep before my head hit the pillow.

Bob shook me awake the next morning, telling me he had already been to the fly shop to coordinate the shuttle service for our pending float trip that day. He also had news: The black caddis hatch was not happening as expected, and the fishing was a hit-or-miss proposition. Oh, well! We came to go fishing, so after a quick breakfast we headed to the Three-Mile Access, dumped the driftboat into the water amid billowing clouds of fog, and prepared for a day on the water. And that's exact what we had—a day on the water with nary a fish to our credit. What a bummer!

That evening when we stopped at the restaurant for dinner, we talked with one of our guide friends, who was already there. That should have been a clue, because this guy is usually one of the last people off the river. Like a lot of guides, he wasn't giving away all of his secrets, but he did mention the fishing was better early in the morning. We thanked him for his tip and headed for the trailer and a night's sleep.

The next morning we arrived at the foggy river a little after six o'clock (two hours earlier than the day before). The only car or trailer in the parking lot belonged our guide friend from the previous evening. His truck had cooled off, indicating that he had arrived at the river an hour or more before we had. Interesting! If we wanted to get to the river tomorrow at the same time he did, we would have to be much earlier.

The day was a repeat of the previous—no fish for me, but Bob did manage to catch a couple of rainbows on a San Juan Worm presented from the boat as we drifted from one location to the next. The fog did finally clear that afternoon, but that didn't improve the fishing.

During the day we had discussed what our options could be, and finding a lot of spent Trico spinners in slack water got us focused in that direction. Over an extended lunch I related to Bob what Gary had shared with me several weeks earlier at the Federation of Fly Fishers Conclave in West Yellowstone, Montana. There he talked about his Clear Wing Spinner and what a great attractor pattern it had proven to be. It was good enough to edge his favorite attractor, the Royal Trude, out of its first-place position in his fly boxes. Understand that I make this statement based on Gary's fly box contents in the early 1990s. Over the years I learned that his fly boxes were an ever-evolving process.) He also talked about an experiment a member of his research team, Justin Baker, had in progress regarding submerged Trico patterns presented when those bugs were prevalent. He told me the experiment did not have any results he could call conclusive, but he felt the idea had real merit. That tidbit of information set Bob off on a riverbank, creative binge; he was mentally designing flies and relating their possibilities to me in the process. We finished our day on the river and returned to the trailer to tie several different versions of submerged Trico patterns. Bob really liked one he called a Trico Emerger, constructed with dubbing and a CDC wing.

The next morning we pulled into the parking lot long before five o'clock to find the place empty. We were the first on the river. Wow! We had beat our friend to the river, and the water was alive with working fish; we could hear them "slurping" through the dark, foggy air. Bob rigged up with an indicator fly and a #20 Trico Emerger on a dropper while I dumped the boat into the water. We launched and had not drifted more than a few yards when Bob let out a whoop and yelled, "Fish on!" I eased the boat over to the side of the river and dropped anchor while Bob fought the fish. In a few minutes he landed a nice rainbow, released it, and prepared to switch positions with me so that I could fish. I was concerned about a cement abutment on the outside of a sharp turn downstream a short distance, and elected to stay on the oars for a while longer. Before I could pull the anchor, Bob was into another fish. By the time we passed the concrete abutment, he had released two more trout and it was my turn to fish. I broke a two-day losing streak in the next few minutes, seducing several fish with a Trico Emerger Bob had tied the previous evening. We settled down to a day of great fishing, or so we thought.

As the sky turned gray and the sun finally peeked over the horizon, the fish just stopped working. Throughout the day we picked up a few fish, all on the Trico Emerger, but it was far from the "grand slam" we had anticipated.

That evening at the trailer we reviewed the day's results and concluded that a sunken version of a Trico did in fact seem to prove more attractive to the fish. I placed a note in my Day Timer to call Gary when I got home to share the experience with him. Somewhere over the next several days, I misplaced the note and forgot about it.

Almost six months later I found it again while going through my documentation/paperwork in preparation for meeting with my accountant to do taxes for the year. The note provided a temporary escape from the dreaded tax project, so I picked up the phone and called Gary. After I related the Bighorn River experience, he chuckled then shared his findings over the past season regarding Justin's submerged Trico adults. Gary concluded by saying that some of the toughest fishing could be when the female Tricos were laying their eggs. At that time the fish tended to hold under the surface, feeding on the drowned adults rather than exposing themselves by eating the spinners on the surface. Gary believed he got better results using a submerged fly rather than a dry one during a heavy Trico spinner fall, and he proceeded to share Justin's new pattern with me—the Drowned Trico.

Over the years I've proven to myself the importance of a submerged fly presented during Trico activity, and the Drowned Trico has proven its worth to me many times over when presented during a hatch or spinner fall. I'm not saying I never use a Trico dry fly any more, but I almost always have a submerged pattern on a dropper under it—especially if the dry is a Clear Wing Spinner. By using this two-fly combo, I've had a LaFontaine "edge up" on the competition, my lovely wife, Gretchen. Unfortunately, she will know my trick after she edits this piece, and I'll be back to looking for another way to outfish her. Oh, well, I'll worry about that later.

Drowned Trico

Hook: Size 18 to 22, 1x long dry fly

Thread: White and black

Tail: Two blue dun hackle fibers, split

Abdomen: White thread

Thorax: Black touch dubbing

Wing: Antron fibers, sparse, thorax length

Step 8.1: Mount the hook in the vise, and attach the tying thread in the center of the shank. Wrap to the end while pulling straight back on the tag end of the thread; this positions it on top of the hook shank. Make sure to leave the tag end long for use in the next step.

Step 8.2: Select two blue dun hackle fibers, and tie them to the back of the hook to form a tail. Secure them with a couple thread wraps. Pull the tag end of the thread between the two fibers to separate them. After achieving the desired separation, anchor the thread to the hook while advancing it back to the center of the hook. Trim off the waste part of the tail and the extra thread.

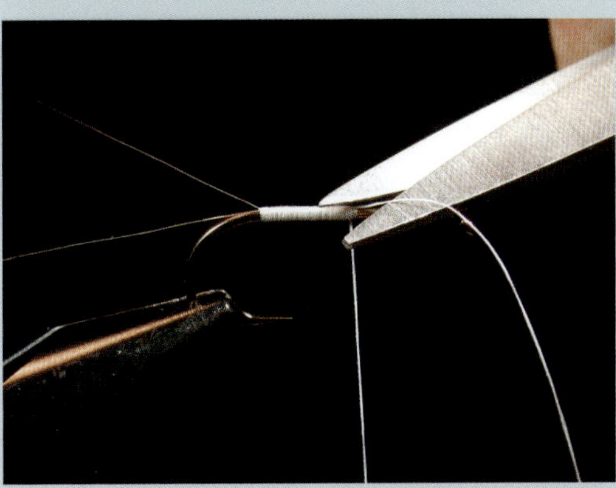

Step 8.3: Whip-finish the white thread and trim it from the hook. Attach black tying thread, trim off the waste end, and coat it with BT's Super Tacky dubbing wax. Apply black touch dubbing to the thread by "patting" the clump to the tacky strand. *Do not* twist the dubbing; instead wrap the thread around the front of the hook to form the thorax. Leave the thread handing near the front of the hook.

Step 8.4: Select a sparse clump of clear Antron fibers, and tie them to the hook to form a wing. Gretchen and I like about eight fibers on a fly smaller than a size 20; the larger illustrated pattern has a few more for clarity's sake.

Step 8.5: Use a pair of scissors to trim the wing short. When we scripted the video, Gary suggested that it should be slightly longer than the back of the thorax.

Step 8.6: Apply a whip-finish, and trim the thread from the hook. A coating of head cement completes the fly.

Chapter 9

Drunken Sailor

When Gretchen and I were working with Gary on one of the first videos we produced for him, he talked at length about "off-balance weighting" in some of his fly patterns. "Off-balancing a fly causes it to react like an injured life form in the water column, thus triggering a kill reaction in the predator fish," advised Gary while we were capturing the footage for the Roll Over Scud. He explained that putting the weight on the side of the fly caused it to travel upright through the water during the strip part of a retrieve, but during the pause part of the same retrieve, the fly would fall on its side. During that session we recorded several of his off-balance flies that already had proven track records. Near the end of the day, he asked us to tie a fly for him based on an idea that had been banging around in his mind's eye for some time. It was an off-balance, marabou-style streamer.

Gary asked us to thoroughly test the pattern in our home waters, while he would have his field staff do so on the rivers near his home in Montana. Al asked, "What is its name?" Gary responded that it didn't have one, but we would think of something if the field team found it to be productive.

On our trip home (at that time in Colorado) we had to drive right by some really great water in southeastern Idaho. We stopped on the lower Henry's Fork near Ashton to send the new lopsided streamer on its maiden voyage. On the first cast I hooked a really nice rainbow. The fish slammed the streamer so hard during the pause part of my retrieve that I almost dropped the fly rod. Of course I lost the fish in the process, but two casts later I wasn't caught unaware and landed the first of several nice trout during the short time we spent fishing.

When we got home we called Gary to report on the great success we had with his unnamed pattern. It turned out that he had a similar report from a couple of fellows on the field team there in Montana. I advised Gary we would spend some time the next day videotaping the fly in the water to see what the action looked like. We used Schweitzer Lake near our home to film the fly in action, me on the camera and Gretchen on the rod. We taped the fly wobbling through the water then falling on its side with the wing suspended above it. The helpless posture it assumed during the pause part of the retrieve seemed to prove attractive to the fish; it was incredible to watch the bluegill in the lake wait for it to pause, fall on its side, and then attack it with abandon.

I decided to try getting the camera nearer to the water's surface to film the action up close. I leaned toward the water, tracking the fly with the camera while Gretchen stripped the line. All of a sudden a large bluegill charged out of the depths, grabbed the fly, and cleared the water with the hook stuck in its mouth. The camera and I were both covered in a shower of water caused by the acrobatic fish, which Gretchen fought and released a few minutes later. After she turned it loose, Gretchen joined me on the bank. I was laughing so hard I couldn't do much more than hand her the camera. She rewound the last footage and checked what it had captured. The tape revealed a dark, shadowy flash followed by an explosion of water that had done a very good job of covering up any action I had hoped to capture. Oh, well, sometimes you can shoot hours of tape to get minutes of usable footage. In this case the footage was useless, but we included it in the sample we forwarded to Gary. He got a good chuckle out of it, and that's all it was worth.

After viewing the test footage, Gary commented that the fly looked like an ancient, drunken sailor stumbling out of a bar on his way back to the ship. The name stuck; however, Gary did caution during one of our conversions to not apply the name to the great people in our modern-day Navy. I couldn't agree more.

Gretchen and I have both learned that *all* of Gary's flies have merit and are useful in a range of applications. Then again, some of his other patterns are "killers" in almost any situation. The Drunken Sailor is such a fly. I recommend that you include it in your fly box—it has a permanent position in mine.

Drunken Sailor

Hook: Size 2 to 10, 3x long streamer
Thread: White or color to match the body
Weight: Two lead strips
Body: Antron yarn, color of choice
Wing: Marabou, color of choice
Hackle: Antron fibers, collar style
Head: Plastic bead; metal bead is too heavy

Gray materials were used in the illustrations rather than white as suggested in the recipe to help provide photographic clarity. However I highly suggest tying this fly in a range of sizes and colors; you won't be disappointed. Also experiment with its construction. Personally I like my Sailors to have eyes added to the bead head. I also often replace the Antron hackle with a regular feather collar of an appropriate color. Please let Gretchen and me know how it works for you; it has been great for us!

Step 9.1: Slip a white plastic bead over the hook point and onto the shank. Place the hook in the vise, then slide the bead forward to meet the eye. Attach white tying thread to the hook behind the bead, and lay down a thread base that covers the complete shank. Bind a strand of lead wire (or nonlead) to the *side* of the hook shank, then top it with a second piece of wire on the *same side.* Be certain to place the second strand of wire on top of the first; it has a tendency to slip under the first rather than stay on top. Whip-finish the thread, and trim it from the hook. Cover the thread wraps with a coating of Aqua Flex, then place the wet assembly in a rotating dryer to cure. In this photograph I've rotated the hook a partial turn toward the camera to better illustrate the wires on top of each other.

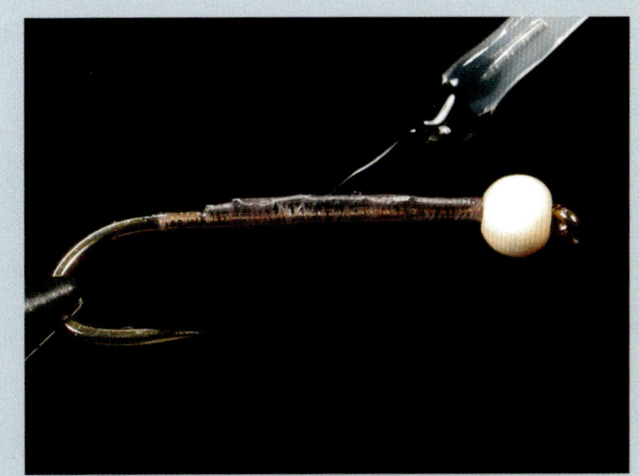

Step 9.2: Once it is dry, place it back in the vise, attach the tying thread, and bind the Antron body material to the top of the hook while wrapping to the end of the shank. Place a half-hitch, then temporarily store this bobbin in a material keeper. Trim any materials as needed.

Step 9.3: For now, attach a second bobbin (black in the photograph) at the front of the hook just behind the plastic bead. Wrap the Antron yarn forward to meet the black thread forming the body, tie it off, and trim the excess materials.

Step 9.4: Select a marabou feather, and tie it to the hook so that it extends beyond the bend. Trim the waste end of the marabou, whip-finish the thread, and clip it from the hook.

Step 9.5: Retrieve the bobbin stored in the material keeper. Separate the marabou strands so that only those near the tip of the feather (back of the fly) are under the control of your left hand. Take a loop of thread between those fibers and the ones in front of them. This loop of thread serves as the first turn in a rib and also anchors the tip part of the feather to the hook.

Step 9.6: Advance the thread forward, forming the rest of the rib and also anchoring the marabou feather to the hook Matuka style. In the illustrated fly, I anchored the feather in four different positions on the hook shank.

Step 9.7: Form a dubbing loop, and center a clump of clear Antron fibers in it. Use a dubbing loop tool to twist the thread/fibers into a fuzzy rope. Start wrapping an Antron hackle collar.

Step 9.8: Make certain to stroke the Antron fibers back after each turn of the collar. Tie off and trim the waste end of the dubbing loop.

Step 9.9: Apply a whip-finish, trim the thread, and coat with Aqua Head to complete the fly.

Enchanted Prince

Each time Gary met with the four of us (Paul, Char, Gretchen, and me) to script the next video, the first words out of his mouth went something like, "How are things?" We soon learned this question was really Gary double-talk that roughly translated to, "Where are you fishing? Did you catch anything? On what?" Then he wanted to know *all* the details: patterns, time of day, weather conditions, etc. His questions were endless and relentless; he was reliving our experiences through our reports.

This day Gary reported with enthusiasm that he had floated a local river near Missoula with a couple of his Montana test team. He wasn't able to fish himself, but he did enjoy riding in the boat and watching his team test patterns. The hot topic of discussion was the Drunken Sailor and the incredible results he reported his team was experiencing. I had to add to that story line with a few experiences of my own where the Sailor was guilty of seducing more than a few Colorado trout (and other fish as well).

In time that story line had been reviewed in enough detail to consider it done and time to move on to the next topic. Gary turned to Paul and Char, who had remained fairly quiet up to this point; just taking notes for future reference. They both started to speak, stopped, and finally Char encourage Paul to continue. Quite frankly he seemed more than a bit hesitant; he finally acknowledged they had been enjoying some great fishing on a well-known Utah river not far from their home. However, they had been enjoying *great* fishing using a well-known pattern with a LaFontaine twist, but it wasn't one of Gary's flies. Gary couldn't have cared less; he wanted to know the whole story, including the pattern's name. Paul said the fly didn't have a name; it was a Prince Nymph with a Double Magic body. Both Paul and Char warmed up to the subject and started describing results that left Gretchen and me speechless. And all Gary could say was, "Where, when, how many, how deep, how...how, time?" etc.

After more than thirty minutes of "grilling," Gary finally asked Paul to tie the fly so that he could see what it looked like. He completed an orange Double Magic Prince Nymph in the next few minutes and passed it around for all to see.

As soon as he saw the fly up close, Gary wanted it in the next video. We had already scripted that video, so we moved the presentation order on several flies to make room for the new pattern. The flies bumped out of rotation were added to future volumes of *LaFontaine Originals*.

Now we had to figure out a name for the new fly. Of course we could have called it Double Magic Prince Nymph, but I wasn't in favor of such a long name—it didn't fit well on the video/DVD title page. Besides, both Paul and Char kind of liked the name Enchanted Prince. Gary loved it, and the fly eventually appeared on the second video.

The story could have ended there for Gretchen and me, but it wasn't the ending, it was a beginning. The Prince Nymph has long been a personal favorite pattern, so it didn't take us long to slip a few of the new flies into our "test pattern" fly box. Flies in that box have only two possible destinations: They could be discarded forever if they didn't prove their worth or graduate to the "further investigation" box.

After a year in that box, the Enchanted Prince landed in our "favorites" box and remains there today. If fact, I just returned to the keyboard after checking my equipment waiting in the truck for me to take it fishing; the "favorite" box has over three dozen Enchanted patterns in it and only three regular Prince Nymphs. That means the Enchanted Prince has captured a major position in my personal angling arsenal. The only trout fly that beats it in my top half dozen is the Enchanted Renegade. Now I wonder why that could be?

So what did Gary think of the fly after his research team had time to give it a good test? Let me share with you a quote from an August 2001 e-mail: "We have looked at flies with Antron on them, and trout have never spooked or shied away from them even in the clearest water. Trout move farther for flies that have the sparkle of Antron. In our preliminary testing with scuba divers, trout move farther to take the Enchanted Prince than they do the standard Prince Nymph. In one three-hour fishing session on the Big Hole River, with results tabulated by scuba divers, the Enchanted Prince outfished the Prince Nymph by $3\frac{1}{2}$ to 2. In general fishing experiences by a wide range of anglers, the Enchanted Prince, with the magic of Antron, seems like a sensational new variation on a classic pattern." I couldn't agree more, as evidenced by my personal fly boxes and on-the-water experience.

Before I tie the fly, I want you to watch for a couple of tips. One is a technique on making the white biot wings more durable; the other is from Gary. Read the last step carefully, and you'll receive a really great tying tip from the master himself. Now let's tie the fly.

Enchanted Prince

Hook: Size 8 to 20, 2x long nymph

Bead: Gold, sized to fit the hook

Thread: Black or color of choice

Wings: White biots, divided

Tail: Brown biots, divided

Body: Peacock herl, orange (color of choice) Antron touch dubbing

Hackle: Brown

Head/collar: Peacock herl

Step 10.1: Slip a bead on the hook, and mount it in the vise. Slide the bead forward to the hook eye, and attach the thread behind it. Wrap to the end of the shank, and trim off the excess thread.

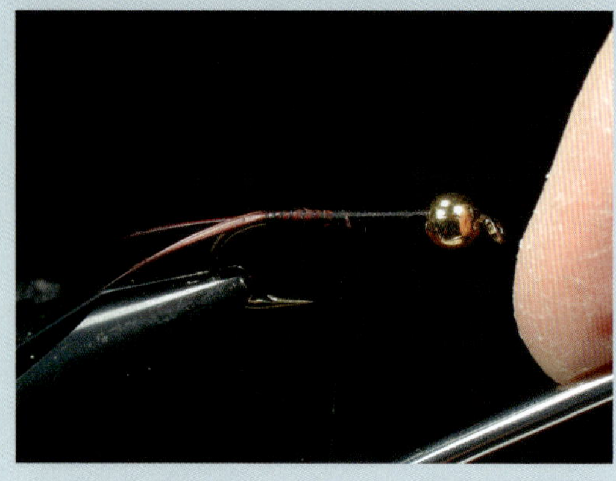

Step 10.2: Select a pair of brown biots (turkey or goose), and tie them to the end of the shank to form a divided tail. (Paul likes his divided tail with the natural curve of the biots pointing down, so I'm illustrating it here in that manner. I like the tail to be equal in length to half of the shank, so again I'm illustrating that proportion.) Trim the waste biots at the middle of the hook.

Step 10.3: Wrap the thread forward to meet the bead. Select two white biots, and tie them to the hook, divided with the tips pointing forward (the bead pushes them up) and the natural curve up. (I like them to be as long as the hook shank.) We'll move them into their final position later. Trim as needed, and wrap the thread to the end of the shank.

Step 10.4: Select several peacock herls, and tie them to the back of the hook by their tips. Apply dubbing wax to about 3 inches of the thread. Pat orange touch dubbing to the tacky thread, allowing the wax to grab as many fibers as it can hold. Form a dubbing loop with the touch-dubbed thread and the peacock herl. Anchor them in an electronics test clip, then rotate it in one direction, forming a piece of Antron high-lighted peacock chenille. Start wrapping the body. Sometimes the waxed thread will grab a large clump of touch dubbing. Use your fingers to remove any excess dubbing before wrapping it into the body. Here I've removed all the larger clumps before starting it.

Step 10.5: Finish wrapping the body, and anchor the peacock chenille with several thread wraps. Trim off the waste. Paul recommends not placing a rib because it tends to mat down the Antron highlights, defeating their original intent.

Step 10.6: Strip the fuzzy material from the base of the stem on a brown hackle feather, tie it to the hook, and wrap a two-turn collar. Trim off the waste end.

Step 10.7: Fold the white biots over, and anchor them in place with several turns of thread, forming the wings. Here's a tip: The natural curve on the wings is pointing down. Anchoring the wings in this manner makes them much less prone to slip from under the thread wraps, consequently producing a more durable fly.

Step 10.8: Tie a single peacock herl to the hook in front of the wings, and wrap a several-turn collar to cover the thread wraps that anchor the wings in place. Trim off the waste part of the herl.

Step 10.9: At this point most of us would apply a whip-finish, trim the thread, and place a drop of head cement. In the process the peacock collar would become matted from the application of glue. Now for Gary's tip: Place the drop of glue *on top of the bead,* then drag the "leading thread" of the whip-finish through the glue while wrapping it into position. Voilà! You now have a cemented whip-finish without matting down the peacock collar. Trim off the thread as needed.

Chapter 11

EZ2C Caddis

*T*his is one of the flies Paul suggested we include in the original video *LaFontaine Originals* while we brainstormed a script over dinner one evening at a fly-fishing show in Grand Junction, Colorado. At the time we had no idea there would be a total of seven volumes in the LaFontaine saga, so we tried to include as many flies as we could into a two-hour VHS tape. The four of us parted company the next morning after breakfast with the understanding we would meet in a few weeks to shoot the actual footage.

At the time of the shoot, I agreed to provide the studio/editing capabilities; Paul would bring fourteen zip-lock bags with the contents needed to tie each pattern. The only pattern for which a tier was lined up to make the on-camera presentation was the Bead Head Marabou Worm, with Paul as presenter. The rest of the patterns needed someone to present them. Long story short, each of us had to practice a fly before turning on the camera and lights. The progress was slow to say the least. On the last day of the shoot, we were down to the last pattern, the EZ2C Caddis, and quite frankly time was running out. I agreed to tie the fly without any practice if Paul would join me off camera, but on a microphone, and tell me how to tie the fly while we filmed it. That was my introduction to the EZ2C Caddis.

Considering our quick introduction, you could understand that the fly and I might go our separate ways after such a short time together, but it wasn't to be. After filming that last pattern, we all were glad to relax for the first time in several days and evenings. We threw all the flies accumulated while filming on the corner of my fly-tying workstation and left them there while we took a well-deserved rest.

The next day Paul and Char left for home, and Gretchen and I headed to the tying room to get fly orders out to customers. Every time I entered the room or let my mind wander, that darned fly crept into my vision. There was something about its color that just wouldn't leave me alone; it kept calling to me. Maybe it was the realization that my eyesight wasn't as good as it had been a few years earlier. I don't know, but it was always in the back of my mind over the next several weeks.

A few months later we were preparing to visit Gretchen's parents in Boise, then do some fishing in central Idaho on our way to Missoula to meet with Gary concerning a possible contract to shoot several more videos for him. At the last minute, as we were packing the car in preparation for the trip, I ran back into the house and grabbed that darned EZ2C Caddis from my workstation and put it in my fly box—just in case I needed it!

After a nice visit with Gretchen's parents, we headed to our favorite fishing spot, the Lochsa River in central Idaho, which just happens to be along Highway 12—the route that would deliver us to Missoula several days later to visit Gary. When we left for the river, we planned on getting food and coffee "somewhere up there" (out of the valley, along the river) not really knowing where "there" would be. When we got to the river, we found that "there" didn't have anything available; stores, etc., just happened to be closed.

On a positive note, the fishing was incredible. And you know what the hot pattern was? If you guessed the EZ2C Caddis, you would have been right. We had only been on the water a short time when I had to stop fishing to tie several more of the patterns on the tailgate of the truck. That evening, after one of our best days on the water in a long time, we fell into bed in the back of the truck so tired we didn't care about missing dinner.

The next morning our hunger was a much more pressing problem than it had been the night before, but the fish were still going crazy like they had the previous day. We fished for a couple of hours, then we finally *had* to do something about food and drink.

We tore the truck apart looking for food and beverage items. We found three old granola bars, one can of Coke, some No-Doze pills, and a thermos of water. Oh, yeah, there was a bush of ripe thimbleberries at the edge of our campsite. So for breakfast Gretchen had a can of Coke, one and a half granola bars, and rounded her meal out with thimbleberries. I had a drink of water with a No-Doze pill (lots of caffeine in that), the rest of the granola bars, and several handfuls of thimbleberries. Folks, I'm here to tell you that it wasn't great, but we did manage to get in several more hours of fishing before we had to leave for Missoula. You never know what you can do to get by until you have to—*or* the fishing is just too darned good to leave. Thankfully I'm lucky enough to have a wife who thought the whole experience was fun; I didn't end up in divorce court like some friends I know might have.

I do have to tell you, though, the first restaurant we saw was like an oasis in a desert. We certainly didn't drive by without stopping for a good, long while!

When we related the story to Gary, I thought he was going to fall off his chair laughing. I guess it's good to negotiate a contract when everyone is in good spirits; at least it worked out well for all of us. The result was six more videos, a lot of fun, and now this book.

EZ2C Caddis

Hook: Size 8 to 20, 1x long standard dry fly

Thread: Olive

Body: Olive dubbing, in two parts

Underwing: Elk hair, stacked

Overwing: Yellow calf tail

Hackle: Grizzly brown mix

Head: Thread

Step 11.1: Mount the hook in the vise, and attach the tying thread about one-third of the shank length back from the eye. Wrap to the end of the shank and back about halfway. Leave the thread there in preparation for the next step. Trim the waste end as needed.

Step 11.2: Apply wax to the thread, then use its tackiness to attach a length of dubbing sufficient to cover the back one-third of the hook. I like to wrap from a point near the center of the hook back on the shank to the end and then forward to the starting position. This process allows me to build a more substantial body with better accuracy than if I try to dub it from the back of the hook forward.

Step 11.3: Select, clean, and stack a clump of elk hair (deer would also work). Tie it to the shank to form an underwing that is long enough to extend to a point slightly past the end of the hook bend. Trim off the waste fibers, then wrap several thread turns to cover them and provide a base for the next step. Don't worry if the hair fibers flare a bit more than needed; we'll take care of that problem in the next step.

Step 11.4: Use dubbing wax to apply another section of the fibers to the thread. Wrap it over the trimmed ends of the underwing. (It will take less dubbing to produce a body equal in size to the back part due to the dimension of the trimmed underwing fibers. Consider that when selecting the quantity of dubbing.) Allow a couple of dubbing-covered thread wraps to climb a short distance onto the elk underwing to bring any overly flared hair fibers under control. After placing this part of the body, advance the thread forward partway onto the bare part of the hook.

Step 11.5: Select, clean, and stack a clump of fluorescent yellow calf tail hair. Tie it to the hook to form a Trude overwing equal in length to the elk hair placed in a previous step. Trim the waste at a severe angle to later provide a tapered hackle platform. Wrap the thread forward almost to the hook eye.

Step 11.6: Slip a strand of thread between the elk and calf tail hair, then apply forward pressure on it to slightly separate the two. This process keeps the stiffer calf tail hair from mashing down the elk underwing. Also, the low angle of the thread tension from the position near the hook eye provides a "pull point" that lifts the hair without cocking it to one side. If the pull point is too close to the base of the calf tail hair, then the overwing will not sit straight on the hook shank.

Step 11.7: Anchor the taut thread there at the front of the hook, then cover-wrap over the trimmed hair fibers to construct the tapered hackle platform. Select brown and grizzly hackle feathers, strip the fuzzy material from the base of their stems, and tie them to the bottom of the hook shank.

Step 11.8: Wrap the brown hackle forward using five semi-open turns, and tie it off at the hook eye. The semi-open turns provide spaces in which to wrap the grizzly hackle in the next step. Trim off the excess brown feather.

Step 11.9: Wrap the grizzly feather forward using seven wraps, filling in the spaces left in the previous step, plus an additional turn in the back and front of the hackle application. If you wrap an equal number of brown and grizzly hackle turns, the darker brown will overpower the grizzly, making the application look like it has much more of the darker color than it really has. Tie off the feather, trim it from the hook, and apply a whip-finish. A coat of head cement will complete the fly.

Chapter 12

EZ2C Mayfly

This particular fly came into Gary's fertile mind long after developing the EZ2C Caddis (see chapter 11). To me it was obviously the product of many hours of research where Gary had time to focus on the pattern, work out problem areas in his mind, and then get a fly tier to assemble it for him. Often that fly tier was his daughter Heather, a member of the Montana research team, or Paul Stimpson. Then he sent the new "test pattern" to his field teams to present it to the real critics—the trout.

If an idea worked, he kept it; if it didn't, it was quickly discarded. Then the process would start over again, incorporating ideas until he got the problems worked out of the new pattern to the point it was time to send it back to the field for more testing. This process continued until early 2000, when Gary finally felt it was time to send the scuba divers into the water to observe this fly in action. He wanted to know why it was working so well.

Interestingly, the answer was similar to that produced from the results of the dive team many years earlier, when they and Gary developed the patterns that went into his incredible book *Caddisflies*. At that time they found Antron to be a key part of the equation—fish seemed to find it very attractive. Years later the EZ2C Mayfly patterns had some of those same characteristics, again created by Antron. Whether Antron was the attraction regarding the EZ2C Mayfly is unknown but, bottom line, the fish really loved them.

The information was perking away in Gary's mind like a pot of coffee ready to boil over, so when I happened to call him to discuss working on another video in early summer 2001, he was ready to explode. And explode he did! He explained about this new fly with an enthusiasm that made me think of a person dancing around the room, except he was confined to a wheelchair at the time. I guess I could say he was as excited as I had ever heard or seen him.

We set a time in early July to meet in Missoula to capture footage on several flies and, most important, the new fly he wanted to show Gretchen and me. As we prepared to close our phone conversation, he asked if his daughter Heather could tie the selected flies. I was delighted to include a tier of her capabilities in the videos and responded, "Yes!" before he could change his mind.

Several days later Gretchen and I arrived in Missoula and rented a suite in one of the area hotels so that we would have enough space to tape the next day. The following morning we had barely finished breakfast when there was a knock on the door. Gary, Heather, and her husband, Patrick, were there to begin work. We had set up the camera, lights, and sound equipment the night before, so everything was ready to go.

Gary was "on task, ready to work," but not before he showed us the new EZ2C Mayfly. After all I had heard about it, I didn't know what to expect, and quite frankly I was a bit disappointed. It didn't look like the fly I had conjured up in my mind's eye. I guess Gary sensed my disappointment, because he started explaining the pattern's features and how he envisioned they attracted the trout. Warming up to this funny-looking critter, I started to really take note of the main items Gary was explaining.

Following is an edited quote from Gary, taken from one of the audiotapes we recorded that day in July 2001: "This fly features a hackle post for visibility without adding additional weight. The body is translucent packing foam wrapped over dubbing. The dubbing is the color of the eggs inside the mayfly, and the foam over body is the color of the insect. The hackle tip wings are extended out over the eye at a 45-degree angle. Because of refraction, when a natural floats down the river, the wings are the first things a feeding trout will see. By exaggerating the angle of the wing, we make this fly even more visible. These three features (the hackle post, the translucent body, and the angled wings) make this an exciting new fly."

The more I looked at it, the more sense it made; Gary's enthusiasm rapidly spread to Gretchen and me. Quoted from the videotape, Gary says: "The fly by the way is doing fabulous. In scuba diving...great...it's a killer." At that point Gary really had our attention, but we set aside our comments in favor of our reason for traveling to Missoula: It was time to capture Heather on camera. We could discuss the fly more at dinner that evening.

Heather moved in front of the camera, I gave the "action" nod, and she started tying and speaking: "Hello, my name is Heather LaFontaine Ellison, and joining me today off camera is my father, Gary LaFontaine, while we tie the..."

I smiled to myself. I've had a lot of experience videotaping untested actors (tiers). Sometimes they do well; other times they fall apart as soon as the red "record light" starts flashing. Heather was a real pro; we completed her footage with almost zero retakes. That doesn't happen very often. Yes, the day was shaping up to be a special one to record in my memory banks; I had a great new fly to think about and a real pro in front of the camera.

I could go on and on about that magical day, including a wonderful dinner with Gary, Heather, and Patrick, but it wouldn't get all of you any closer to a really great (and innovative) fly pattern. And that's my real purpose here; we'll leave the reminiscing to another time and place.

Before we tie this fly, it's important to explain the color choices in the pattern recipes below. They are the color combinations Gary developed, and he considered them *essential* to the pattern's success rate. What makes this fly so productive, I really don't know. But I long ago learned that it's not good to mess with success, so I haven't. I'm listing all of Gary's recipes for you to incorporate into your EZ2C Mayfly patterns. Gretchen and I follow them religiously; you may want to as well.

Blue-Winged Olive (EZ2C)

Hook: Size 16 to 18, 1x long standard dry fly
Thread: Olive
Wings: Dark dun rooster hackle tips
Tail: Dark dun rooster hackle barbs
Post: White rooster hackle (one size larger than hook size)
Rib: Olive thread
Overbody: Packing foam colored olive
Underbody: Olive touch dubbing
Hackle: Dark dun rooster (V-clipped on bottom)

Callibaetis (EZ2C)

Hook: Size 12 to 16, 1x long standard dry fly
Thread: Yellow
Wings: Blue dun rooster hackle tips
Tail: Blue dun rooster hackle fibers
Post: White rooster hackle (one size larger than hook size)
Rib: Yellow thread
Overbody: Packing foam colored olive
Underbody: Medium green touch dubbing
Hackle: Blue dun rooster (V-clipped on bottom)

Gray Drake (EZ2C)

Hook: Size 10 to 12, 1x long standard dry fly

Thread: Olive

Wings: Medium gray rooster hackle tips

Tail: Medium rooster hackle barbs

Post: White rooster hackle (one size larger than hook size)

Rib: Yellow thread

Overbody: Packing foam colored gray

Underbody: Medium green touch dubbing

Hackle: Medium gray rooster (V-clipped on bottom)

Light Cahill (EZ2C)

Hook: Size 12 to 14, 1x long standard dry fly

Thread: Light yellow

Wings: Light ginger rooster hackle tips

Tail: Light ginger rooster hackle barbs

Post: White rooster hackle (one size larger than hook size)

Rib: Yellow thread

Overbody: Packing foam colored yellow

Underbody: Pale yellow touch dubbing

Hackle: Light ginger rooster (V-clipped on bottom)

Pale Morning Dun (EZ2C)

Hook: Size 16 to 18, 1x long standard dry fly

Thread: Yellow

Wings: Light dun rooster hackle tips

Tail: Light dun rooster hackle fibers

Post: White rooster hackle (one size larger than hook size)

Rib: Yellow thread

Overbody: Packing foam colored yellowish olive

Underbody: Yellow touch dubbing

Hackle: Light dun rooster (V-clipped on bottom)

Step 12.1: Set the hook in the vise, and attach the tying thread just behind the hook eye. Wrap several turns back and then back forward to the eye. Trim off the waste part of the thread. Cut a narrow strip of clear packing foam, and use an olive felt-tip marker to color one side. Set it aside to dry and use in a future step. Notice the mottled, buggy appearance the marker and foam produce. Also, I've clipped a point at the end of the strip that I'll eventually tie to the back of the hook.

Step 12.2: Select two dun hackle tips, and tie them to the hook at the eye pointing forward to form the wings. They should be equal to about 75 percent of the hook shank in length. Trim off the waste part of the feathers, and save them to use later.

Step 12.3: Wind to the center of the hook, select several dun hackle fibers, and tie them to the hook while wrapping to the end of the shank. Wrap back to the center of the hook, and trim any waste fibers. Pull the thread back, under the new tail, and forward again to the center of the hook. This maneuver will tilt the tail up slightly while remaining "in line" with the shank because I'm pulling on the thread from the center of the hook. If I complete this process too far back on the shank, the tail with not be "in line" with the hook.

Step 12.4: Select a white hackle feather one size larger than the hook in the vise. Strip the fuzzy material from the base of the stem, then tie it to the shank with the tip pointing forward (the stem is buried in the body). Wrap several *tight* turns of hackle in front of the thread, making certain the last wrap is against the strand. Tie it off, and trim the waste part of the feather, leaving the thread hanging just behind the wrapped hackle.

Step 12.5: Pull all the wrapped fibers above the shank, and take two crisscross wraps under them to force the hackle to remain on top of the hook. Now take one or two turns around the fibers to form them into a bundle—or, as Gary calls it, "a parachute post," which is really a "visibility beacon" on top of the hook. If you don't have a white feather, a light-colored grizzly is a good substitute.

Step 12.6: Form a dubbing loop while wrapping to the back of the hook. Clip one side of the loop to form a single strand to later use as a rib.

Step 12.7: Retrieve the colored foam prepared in the first step, and tie it to the hook by its tip end. Be certain the colored side is facing down.

Step 12.8: Treat a 2-inch section of thread with wax, then pat the tacky strand with green touch dubbing. *Do not* twist it into a noodle. Wrap the dubbed thread around the hook to later represent the eggs inside the female's body.

Step 12.9: Wrap the foam forward over the touch dubbing to complete the body. Be sure to let some of the touch dubbing stick out between the turns of foam. Also notice that the colored side of the foam that was facing down turns to the top on its first forward wrap. Tie off, and trim the excess foam.

Step 12.10: Retrieve the rib (former dubbing loop) material, and counter-wrap it over the body. The reverse wrap is needed to strengthen the fragile foam.

Step 12.11: Finish wrapping the rib, tie it off, and trim the excess. Retrieve the two hackle feathers remaining from the first step, strip the fuzzy material from the base of the stems, and tie them to the hook behind the "visibility post." Wrap each feather one turn behind the post and three in front. Tie them off, and trim the surplus.

Step 12.12: Apply a whip-finish, and trim off the thread. Use a thumbnail to force the wings up at a 45-degree angle, making certain they are also divided. The last function is to clip a V in the bottom of the hackle.

Chapter 13

EZ2C Midge

*W*here would you like to go to dinner?" I asked the group that included Gary LaFontaine; his daughter Heather; her husband, Patrick; and my lovely wife, Gretchen, after a long day's work. They all deferred to Gary. I knew before he opened his mouth to speak where we were headed. "Mack, of course," he responded, meaning Mackenzie River Pizza Company, not far from our hotel in Missoula.

I don't know why I bothered to ask; he chose that restaurant more often than any other. Not that I didn't like pizza; I thought it was a great idea for a meal at least two or three times a year. Oh, well, I knew I could look forward to a really fun evening and figured I better keep my notebook and pen close by; Gary had been in rare humor all day. The evening promised to be even better. And it was!

After ordering our pizzas I returned to the table to rejoin a conversation regarding the EZ2C Mayfly, a pattern we had filmed that day. All of us were excited about its possibilities, speculating what the feedback would be once *LaFontaine Originals,* Volume IV, went on sale. A couple of beverages just fueled the synergy that had started earlier in the day and moved on into the evening.

Usually early after dinner, Gary would indicate it was time for him to get back to his managed-care facility, Patrick and Heather would load him in the van, and the evening would be over. Something was different tonight. An hour after dinner, Gary was still going strong; another hour, and nothing had changed. Gary was on a roll, and all of us just climbed on for the ride.

Around ten o'clock Gary turned to me and asked if I was ready to discuss more business. I answered to the affirmative as both Gretchen and I reached for our notepads. We were back on task, and Gary was the taskmaster. He wanted to know how soon I could edit *Volume IV* and have it ready for sale. I gave him a date (I think it was a couple of weeks) when I would have a preliminary copy for him to review. We agreed on the timeline and kind of hit a lull in the conversation.

I could see the evening ending in the next few minutes and wanted to ask one more question. "Gary, we need two more EZ2C patterns to round out the video series," I started, "a midge pattern and a stonefly pattern." He kind of grinned and said he'd been thinking the same thing, and right there at the table he started "creating" an EZ2C Midge. The stonefly would have to wait for another time.

Gary employed a similar wing as the one used on the Diving Egg-Laying Midge in *LaFontaine Originals,* Volume III, and a black body constructed like the EZ2C Mayfly we had filmed that day. Up to this point it sounded really good. Earlier in the evening I had shared some of my experiences fishing a Bi-Visible fly as a young boy in the waters around my home in Iowa. Gary took the Bi-Visible concept and applied it to our hackle need for "this midge pattern in progress." He suggested a black hackle fronted by several turns of a white feather. It sounded good to Gretchen and me. We promised to tie several samples of the new pattern when we got home and test them on the Gunnison River not far from where we lived at that time in Colorado.

The day after we returned home, while I cleaned off the answering machine and returned business calls, Gretchen tied several EZ2C Midges. When I completed that part of my work and joined her in the tying room, I could tell she wasn't pleased with something. "I can't see the white hackle on the Bi-Visible part of this fly," she said. "Two turns [of hackle] just isn't enough." She was right; it didn't show up like it had in our mind's eye during our conversation with Gary at the restaurant a few days before. I started work on a long overdue order of flies while she continued to ponder the problem.

Several flies later she had the problem solved. On flies size 16 or 18, four turns of black and four turns of white made the fly look like it only had about half as many turns of light over dark—just the appearance we discussed with Gary. On smaller sizes down into the 20s, she kept the same percentage of each hackle color, using fewer turns as the fly size was reduced. We shared our findings with Gary via e-mail, and after reviewing the patterns we sent him, he agreed. In a follow-up e-mail he stated, "...more turns of white to offset the darker black hackle" seemed to do the job.

Now that we had the pattern looking the way we thought it should, it was time to test it using a known pattern (a Griffin's Gnat) as a benchmark. On three different days we presented the EZ2C Midge and a Griffin's Gnat on a two-fly rig to trout in the Gunnison River. I can say neither pattern was better or worse than the other; they both seemed to produce a fairly equal number of fish.

However, both of us, who are getting a little older, could definitely seen the EZ2C Midge much better than the benchmark pattern. I know in my case, every fish I caught on the Griffin's Gnat I had hooked when I saw a rise "near" my EZ2C Midge. In other words, the EZ2C was acting as my "strike indicator"—after a distance of 40 feet, I just couldn't see the Griffin's Gnat at all.

Today I have several Griffin's Gnats in my fly box and nearly a dozen EZ2C Midges. They are both great patterns, but I can see one better than the other. You'll need to make your choice of which pattern to use based on your personal needs. I sure know which one we'll select!

EZ2C Midge

Hook: Size 16 to 24, 1x long standard dry fly

Thread: Black

Rib: Black thread

Underbody: Black touch dubbing

Overbody: Packing foam colored black

Wing: Clear Antron, looped

Rear hackle: Black

Front hackle: White

Step 13.1: Mount the hook in the vise, and attach the tying thread to the shank about one-third back from the eye. Apply a thread base that extends to the end of the shank. Be sure to leave a long tag of thread; don't trim it from the hook.

Step 13.2: Use a pair of scissors to cut a section of packing foam that is as wide as half the hook gape and about 3 inches long. Clip a tapered point on one end. Use a black felt-tip marker to color one side of the foam.

Step 13.3: Tie the pointed end of the foam to the back of the hook with the colored side facing down. When I make the first wrap of foam, the colored side will turn itself up (out) as it is wound into position.

Step 13.4: Use a tacky wax to attach black touch dubbing to the thread; *do not* twist it into a noodle. Start wrapping the covered thread forward to form the underbody. (I've used gray touch dubbing to better illustrate this part of the process, because black does not show up well against the background I'm using in the photograph.)

Step 13.5: Finish wrapping the underbody. Use your fingers to remove any excess dubbing. Wrap the packing foam forward to meet the thread. Make certain the black side is facing up/out, and allow some of the underbody to show between the turns of foam. Tie it off, and trim the excess. Counterwrap the rib forward over the body, tie it off, and trim the waste end.

Step 13.6: Select a sparse strand of clear Antron yarn, and tie it to the top of the shank to form a looped Trude-style wing. Adjust its length so that it is no longer than the end of the body. Trim the waste ends at a severe angle, then wrap over them to provide a tapered hackle platform between the wing and the hook eye.

Step 13.7: Strip the fuzzy material from the base end of a black feather, tie it to the hook, and place several turns of hackle (the number is based on the hook size). Tie it off and trim the surplus.

Step 13.8: Repeat the process with a white hackle in front of the black. Make certain to apply at least as much white hackle as black. Tie it off, and trim the waste.

Step 13.9: Apply a whip-finish, and trim the thread from the hook. A coating of head cement completes the fly.

Chapter 14

EZ2C Stonefly (February Red)

"Hey, Al, are you having any trouble with the color on these midge patterns?" Gretchen shouted at me across the water. "Yeah!" I answered back as I walked toward her. We were on the Gunnison River near Pleasure Park, Colorado, testing the EZ2C Midges for Gary. The flies still seemed to be attractive to the trout, but they certainly were losing the color we had placed using a black felt-tip marker earlier that day at the vise. "I've been touching mine up with a Sharpie here streamside," I advised Gretchen. "I forgot to leave it in the tying room this morning when we finished tying flies." As I handed the felt-tip pen to her, she made an offhand comment about keeping her in the dark. We finished the day on the river by passing the Sharpie back and forth to keep our patterns touched up. Thankfully, a size 20 fly doesn't have much area that needed attention.

While preparing dinner at home that evening, we discussed the problem. "Do you think we could dye the packing foam?" Gretchen asked. "I don't know, it may not be very easy," I responded. I explained that I had tried dying packing foam a number of years earlier using Rit Dye, and it had been a dismal failure. We decided to give it another try the next morning using a better-quality product than I had used in the past.

As things will often happen, the project got set aside for more pressing needs, and we didn't get back to it until Sunday morning a couple weeks later. We woke up to a steady rain and decided to stay in rather than go out. When I wandered into the kitchen to see what she was doing, Gretchen already had a couple containers of water heating on the stove with a clip-on thermometer attached to each. She mixed scarlet dye in one and black in the other, stirring to dissolve the powder.

When the dye baths each reached 145 degrees Fahrenheit, she placed wide strips of packing foam in each, used white vinegar to set the dye, and allowed each bath to cool. A couple hours later the foam strips were ready to come out of the bath and into the washing tank. They looked good until the rinse water hit them. The black ended up looking like a mixture of gray and white mud, while the scarlet looked like bloodshot lung material. It really looked gross!! Enough said in that regard. We decided that dying the stuff just wasn't going to work.

We spent the rest of the day trying different colored felt-tip marking pens. Some colors and manufacturers produced better results than others, but they all faded, some faster than others.

Next we tested the foam strips with a head-cement coating over the colored portion of the strip. It looked great until we tried to tie the foam on the hook. When we place the strip under tension, the stretching action caused the coating to crack and eventually fall off. It needed to stretch! We needed flexible cement and tried Dave's. It did a great job on some types of packing foam; others just curled up with some type of chemical reaction. Then Gretchen grabbed a bottle of Aqua Flex, a product we distribute. It's flexible and water based. It worked great, making the foam strips colorfast and flexible. The problem was solved.

We prefer telling a customer (or boss) about a problem when we also have the solution. Our e-mail to Gary provided both to a problem he was dealing with himself; his test teams had experienced the same color difficulty we had. Bottom line, we ended up with a solution and added another customer for our Aqua product line—Gary's company, the Book Mailer. Today the Book Mailer is one of our largest Aqua Flex customers. Life is funny sometimes; you never know what turn in the road may appear ahead.

I'll bet those of you reading these words are wondering, "Aren't Al and Gretchen going to tell us about fishing with the EZ2C Stonefly?" No, we're not. If you don't have confidence in the patterns that Gary developed by now, a few more words written by us certainly won't change your mind. Quite frankly, that's what happened to Gretchen and me. By the time we had progressed to this fly, which was released to the public in *LaFontaine Originals,* Volume V, we had gone through an evolutionary process starting with "disbelief," then "skepticism," followed by "wonder," to "grudging acceptance," and finally to "total conversion" to the LaFontaine doctrine. It took time to bring us around, but that talented man could solve angling problems better than anyone either of us had ever met. We were expert fly fishers! Right! It took us a while to understand that there were experts like us, and then there were *experts* like Gary LaFontaine, who was very knowledgeable in his own right and also had an incredibly memory. He always listened to what people had to say and often learned from them.

So back to your question. "No, I'm not going to tell you about the fishing." Just accept that it's a LaFontaine pattern, which means it wouldn't be here if it didn't produce fish. I went through the learning process with Gary in my own way, and you'll have to travel your road as you see fit. I also must admit that Gretchen was a convert much quicker than I was. Paul and Char were already converts when we met them. I guess I'm a slow learner with a hard head! Oh, well, whatever the case may be, let's tie the fly.

EZ2C Stonefly (February Red)

Hook: Size 16, 1x long standard dry

Thread: Brown

Rib: Brown thread

Tail: Pheasant tail fibers, split and short

Underbody: Brown touch dubbing

Overbody: Packing foam colored brown on one side

Foam coating: Aqua Flex

Wing: Dark brown elk hair (deer hair is a good substitute)

Post hackle: White, oversize

Hackle: Brown

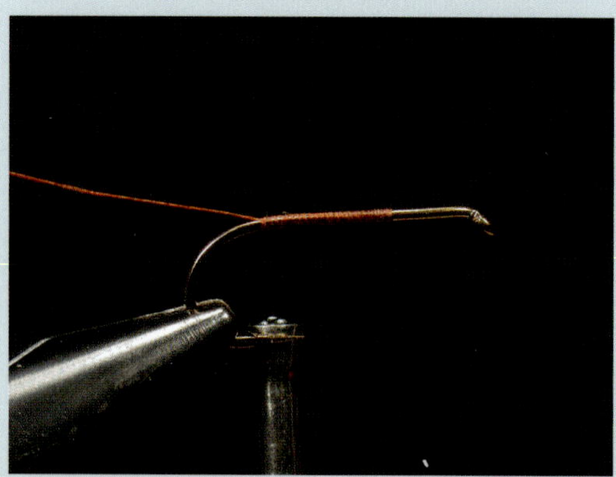

Step 14.1: Place the hook in the vise, and attach the tying thread to it about one-third of the shank length back from the eye. Wrap to the end of the shank, making certain to leave a long "tag end" of thread remaining. Do not cut it from the hook; store it in a material spring for future use.

Step 14.2: Cut a fairly wide strip of packing foam, and color one side of it with a brown felt-tip marker. Allow it to dry, then coat the colored side with Aqua Flex. I like to use a homemade brush assembled from a toothpick and a clump of stacked deer hair. Use a pair of scissors to cut a strip of foam as wide as half the span of the hook gape. The brush and this strip are both illustrated in the photograph.

Step 14.3: Pull a clump of pheasant tail fibers from the feather, and tie them to the hook to form a tail equal to half the hook in length. Trim the waste as needed. (Once Gary suggested splitting the tail but neglected to mention it again. Also, he didn't discuss splitting the tail when we reviewed the fly in our "scripting session." When we shot the video, Gretchen did not split the tail, nor have I in this illustration. It's your choice; I haven't found a need to do so on my personal fishing flies and found no evidence that Gary did either.)

Step 14.4: Finish clipping the strip of brown packing foam from the mother section. Trim a point at one end, then tie it to the hook shank, colored side down. Leave the thread hanging at the back of the hook in preparation for the next step.

Step 14.5: Treat the thread with a tacky dubbing wax. Pat a clump of brown touch dubbing to the tacky thread (don't twist the dubbed thread), then wrap an underbody as illustrated.

Step 14.6: Wrap the colored foam forward over the dubbing placed in the last step. Allow the underbody fibers to show between the turns of colored foam. Tie off the foam, and trim the waste end. Counterwrap the rib over the body, tie it off, and trim the waste end.

Step 14.7: Select a clump of deer or elk hair, clean out the underfur, and even the tips in a stacker. Tie them to the hook to form a Trude-style wing long enough to reach the center of the tail. Trim off the waste fibers at a severe angle, then wrap the thread over them to form a tapered hackle platform. Leave the thread at the start of the wing application.

Step 14.8: Strip the fuzzy material from the base of a white hackle feather that is one size larger than the hook in the vise. Tie it to the hook at the front of the wing, and wrap it several times close together. Tie it off, and trim the surplus. Pull the wrapped fibers up into a "visibility post," and anchor them in place with several of thread wraps, first under and then around the fibers. Leave the thread behind the post.

Step 14.9: Tie a prepared brown hackle to the hook behind the white post. Bind the stem to the shank while wrapping forward to the eye. Wrap the hackle forward to meet the thread, tie it off, and clip the waste end. Apply a whip-finish, and trim the thread from the hook. A drop of head cement will complete the fly.

Chapter 15

Flex Damsel

What environment comes to mind when you think of damselflies (adult or nymphs)? For me it used to be still water until we spent time with Gary preparing to shoot *LaFontaine Originals*, Volume III. Then I learned that they also inhabit some moving water like the mossy back bays on some spring creeks and even slower moving rivers.

Up until the time we discussed the Flex version of this fly, it is a pattern I had basically dismissed. For years I don't think I had a single adult in my vest. I had some patterns that probably suggested the nymph version but never presented them as damsel nymph. I just happened to catch fish on them and never really knew why.

Then I had the chance to learn from Gary why he liked and often used the Flex Damsel. "With the slightest twitch the body bends, and this makes the fly look like a living natural," explained Gary one afternoon. "A suspicious fish will be perched under the Flex Damsel or Dragon, staring up, and then the fly kicks and bends in the middle. That fish will immediately lose all sense of caution and attack the imitation." That last part about "attack the imitation" really got my attention. The way he described it kind of sent chills up my spine.

That night in the motel room, Gretchen and I tied several of the blue Flex Damsels to represent an egg-laying adult and a couple of the gray to mimic a newly hatched teneral. According to Gary, both were quite attractive to the fish; we hoped to find out before too many hours passed.

The next morning we checked out of our motel and left Missoula, headed for our home in Colorado with a slight detour to visit friends in Bozeman. They lived a couple of blocks from the address where our home had been when we lived in that beautiful Montana community. We were looking forward to seeing them again and seeing our "old stomping grounds." When we arrived at their address, we found a note on the door that said, "Gone fishing." We knew that meant they were "catching a few" at a local pond we all often frequented together.

A few minutes later we arrived at water's edge to see their truck parked by the wire gate. The warm afternoon air brought a cry of delight as John used his net to help Sue land a nice rainbow. That brought a smile to our faces as we pulled our equipment from the back of the truck and prepared to join them.

"What are you going to use?" Gretchen asked as she browsed through her fly box. "I'm going to try one of Gary's Flex Damsels," I responded, handing her one of the patterns we had tied the previous evening in Missoula. She didn't reach for it when I tried to pass the fly to her because she was wiggling her vest around trying to get it to set straight, so I just tied the fly to her tippet out of habit. I guess once a guide, always a guide.

She headed down the bank a short distance while I got out my rod, tied on a Flex Damsel, slid the box of flies in my vest, and nestled the multipocketed contraption into position over my shoulders. My dog, Dubbin, was waiting for me to get ready so that we could get started fishing when Gretchen let out a yelp, indicating she was into a fish. I turned around to ask if she needed help in time to see "my" dog headed down the bank in her direction and a rainbow hovering out of the water at the pinnacle of its jump. Wow! What a picture to file away in deep recesses of my memory banks. Then her line went slack. The fish was gone, so I turned back to my own part of the world and finished tying on the fly. Dubbin returned to my side and sat down, waiting to go fishing. As I've mentioned before, he usually stayed with me unless someone was catching more fish than I was, then would abandon me in a flash. Yes, Dubbin was a "loyal" fly-fishing dog.

On my third or fourth cast, I caught a fairly nice fish, followed by another, bigger trout several presentations later. Four more fish and Gretchen was there by my side, asking for another fly. She explained that it was my fault she lost "that nice fish" because I had tied the knot poorly. I doubted that was the case (how could a guide tie a bad knot?), but it wasn't worth further discussion. I reached for the box of Flex Damsels I had placed in my vest. It wasn't there! Wrong pocket! Nope! The other side! Nope!

I took off the vest and went through every pocket several times but couldn't find the box. I went back to the truck, thinking I had dropped it nearby, but I could not find the elusive box of flies. Oh, well, I thought I'd find it soon, so I unclipped the one I had on my tippet and handed it to her. Off she went, while I searched for the box of flies. I kept an eye open all afternoon for that darned box and never did locate it; the rest of my day was a bit slow. On the other hand, Gretchen enjoyed a great afternoon catching numerous fish. My box of flies was gone forever, but I would certainly replace those Flex Damsels as soon as we got home; it was too good a pattern to not have a few with me at all times. Don't you find it amazing how quickly a person can change his perspective; I went from no damselfly patterns in my box to the Flex Damsel becoming a "must-have fly" in one afternoon.

At home after tying a bunch (several dozen) of replacement flies, I placed them in a box and took them to the truck to place them in my vest. I popped open the truck's canopy door, dropped the tailgate, and slid my wader/gear bag toward me. Something fell on the ground after bouncing off my foot. I looked under the truck to see what it was, and there was the "lost" box of flies I thought I had slid into my vest. It must have been hiding under by gear bag all the time I was looking for it. Have you ever noticed when you really, really need something you can't find it? That was certainly the case in this situation, so let's tie the fly so that we both have one just in case it is needed later.

Flex Damsel

Rear Section

Hook: Size 10 to 16, ringed eye

Thread: Blue or gray

Tail: Black Antron, short and combed

Body: Foam (blue or gray), folded over top and bottom

Rib: Copper wire

First wing: Clear Antron

Front Section

Clip: Small Flex Clip

Thread: Blue or gray

Second wing: Calf tail, stacked

Body: Foam (blue or gray), folded over top and bottom

Hackle: Black or dark olive

Head: Trimmed foam

Gray materials were used in the illustrations rather than white as suggested in the recipe to help provide photographic clarity.

Step 15.1: Place a ring-eye hook in the vise, and attach the tying thread to the shank at a position one-third back from the eye. Wrap to the end of the shank. Select a clump of black Antron yarn, and tie it to the hook to form a tail. Trim it so that the tail is equal to the hook gape in length. Use a fine-tooth comb to open and fuzz the Antron fibers. Here, I used gray instead of black Antron for the tail for illustration purposes only; it provides better detail in the photograph against a black background.

Step 15.2: Cut a strip of blue foam (gray if you are tying a teneral) from a bulk piece of the material about as wide as the hook gape. Cut it in half to form two sections, then trim a point on one end of each. Tie the pointed ends to the hook shank, one on the top and the other on the bottom. Clip a several-inch section of copper wire, and tie it to the back of the hook to later use as a rib. Store it in a material spring for now.

Step 15.3: Pull the top piece of foam over the hook, and tie it to the front. Repeat the process on the bottom, then trim both. Make certain to leave room for a wing in the next step. Recover the copper wire from the material spring, and wrap it forward over the body to form a rib. Tie it off, and trim the surplus.

Step 15.4: Select a clump of clear Antron, and tie it to the hook to form a wing. Trim it even with the end of the tail, apply a whip-finish, and clip the thread from the hook. Use a fine-tooth comb to open and fuzz the Antron fibers.

Step 15.5: Remove the hook from the vise, slip a short Flex Clip through the eye, then anchor it in the jaws. Attach the thread at the back of the clip, using several wraps to close the back loop. Wrap to the front, and close that loop as well. Wrap to the back of the clip, leaving the thread there for the next step. Coat the thread with head cement.

Step 15.6: Select, clean, and stack a clump of calf hair (tail or body). Tie it to the clip to form a wing that extends back even with end of underwing formed in a previous step. Trim the waste ends. Wrap the thread over the trimmed hair to a position just behind the front loop.

Step 15.7: Cut two strips of foam as wide as those used in the body. Again trim a point on one end of each, and tie them to the clip. Prepare a black or dark olive hackle, and tie it to the clip in preparation for the next step.

Step 15.8: Wrap the hackle forward over the clip to meet the thread at the front just behind the loop. Tie it off, and trim away the surplus.

Step 15.9: Pull the bottom foam forward, tie it off, and trim the excess. Repeat the process with the top piece of foam. Trim this section of foam a bit longer to form the head. Apply a whip-finish, then trim the thread from the hook. A coating of head cement will complete the fly. (Remember to also tie this fly using gray foam to represent the teneral.)

Chapter 16

Flex Dragon

osquitoes are basically not a trout food but are important to their diet," advised Gary during one of our meetings. He had just spent more than an hour explaining to all of us how dogs were domesticated. That comment sounded like a great bit of information, but my business side was urging me to steer the conversation back to our topic at hand—scripting the next video, not spending more time listening to a story. I asked myself, *Do I stop the flow of information or keep quiet and maybe learn a valuable tidbit that could serve us all well at another time?* My curiosity got the better of me. I sat back to learn about mosquitoes, not knowing I would need the information sooner than I thought.

Gary turned to me and said, "Al, do you remember when we fished 'the ponds' together?" I responded, "Yes, sure I do. I remember the fishing was great and the mosquitoes were horrendous. I think they [the mosquitoes] were worse there than those I encountered in the Mekong Delta in the late 1960s. They seemed to eat 100 percent DEET for lunch!" He chuckled and agreed they were the price a person had to pay to catch fish like we had. Then he guided the conversation right back to the video script when he asked, "Do you remember the damsel- and dragonflies?" I remembered there had been thousands of them and that we had worked a good portion of the day testing patterns to imitate first the damselflies and then, more important, the larger the dragonflies.

It seemed it was an "ask Al day" when Gary again questioned me, "Do you remember how to tell the difference between an adult damselfly and dragonfly?" "The dragonfly is bigger," I answered, knowing darn well that wasn't the response he wanted. He agreed that the adult dragonfly was indeed larger but explained that when it was "at rest," the wings stuck out from the body like those on an airplane. On the other hand, except for a very few exceptions, the smaller adult damselfly's wings were positioned along the body when it was at rest. His gentle reminder set off the "lightbulb over my head" as the memory of that long-ago day flooded back into my consciousness.

He had one more question for me: "Do you remember why we were trying to imitate the dragonfly adults rather than the damselfly?" I answered, "Because those fish had attained their huge size by focusing on the larger dragonflies as their main, high-test food source rather than on their smaller (fewer calories) cousins, the damselflies." My answer was partly true, so Gary let my response slide.

Gary finally let me off the hook when he turned to the group and asked, "What do you think is a major food source for damselfly and dragonfly adults?" I still remember Paul kind of raising his hand, then blurting out, "Mosquitoes?" "Yes!" Gary agreed enthusiastically. He then went on to explain the relationship (as he understood it) between mosquito larvae/adults, damselfly/dragonfly nymphs/adults, and trout. It was a very interesting several minutes. I was glad I hadn't steered him away from "another story," because he brought us back to the video script himself when he told us about his Flex Damsel and Flex Dragon patterns. I started taking notes, thankful I had taped the conversation to better remember it later.

Over the years, as the wiggle concept crept into his bag of tricks, Gary had fashioned several versions of Flex Damsels and Dragons. All were better options than the standard patterns we had used years before on "the ponds," but it took him several years to develop the final version you see here and in the previous chapter.

I realize the patterns you see illustrated on these pages may not represent the pattern profile we've always thought these two insects should display, but Gary felt that the flies (as you see them) have "triggers" built into their design that make them very successful. I'm not sure what part of the fly constitutes a trigger, but using the vernacular of a guy like me, "They may not look like the natural, but they darned sure catch fish! Who cares what they look like if they do the job?" And they certainly do the job and more.

Besides being larger, the Flex Dragon is similar to its cousin, but with a couple of differences. Let's take a look.

Flex Dragon

Rear Section

Hook: Size 6 to 8, ringed eye

Thread: Brown

Rib: Copper wire

Overbody: Foam (brown or olive)

Front Section

Clip: Medium Flex Clip

Thread: Brown

First wing: Stacked hair (brown or olive)

Head: Foam (brown or olive)

Hackle: Brown or grizzly dyed olive

Second wing: Clear Antron

Eyes: Melted monofilament

Head: Brown ostrich herls or peacock herls, your choice

Step 16.1: Set the hook in the vise, and lay down a thread base that covers most of the shank, making certain to leave space at the front to tie down two strips of bulky foam in a future step. Select a clump of pheasant tail fibers, and tie them to the hook to form a tail equal to the span of the gape in length. Trim the waste as needed. Select a 1-inch section of monofilament (I used fifty-pound test), place it in a pair of Sure Grip Tweezers (they stay closed until forced open), and use a flame to melt a set of eyes. I like to finish my eyes with a couple of coats of black fingernail polish, as illustrated in the photograph. Set the eyes aside to dry, leaving them in the tweezers so that the uncured fingernail polish does not become misshapen if accidentally rubbed against the tabletop.

Step 16.2: Trim a fairly long strip of foam that is about as wide as the hook gape, cut it in half, and clip a point on one end of each piece. Tie the pointed ends to the hook, one on top and the other on the bottom. Select a strand of copper wire, and tie it to the hook to later use as a rib.

Step 16.3: Strip one strand out of a four-segment piece of brown Antron yarn, tie it to the hook, and wrap an underbody that ends slightly behind the hook eye. Tie it off, and trim the excess.

Step 16.4: Fold both strips of foam over to cover the top and bottom of the hook. Anchor each at the front of the hook near the eye, then trim off the waste parts. Wind the copper wire forward over the foam to complete the back part of the body. Tie off the wire, and trim it from the hook. Apply a whip-finish, trim off the thread, and dab a drop of head cement to complete this part of the fly.

Step 16.5: Remove the hook from the vise, and connect the Flex Clip to it. Place the clip in the vise with the hook positioned along the back of the jaws to keep it safely out of the way. Attach the thread at the front of the clip, and use several thread wraps to close the front loop. Wrap the thread to the back of the clip, and use several more wraps to close the back loop. A drop of head cement is a good idea to further anchor the thread in place.

Step 16.6: Select a clump of hair, clean out the underfur, and even the tips in a stacker. I used natural brown elk mane, but dyed deer or elk will work equally well. Tie it to the back of the clip to form a wing long enough for the fibers to reach the end of the tail on the trailing hook. Trim off the waste ends, then cover them with several turns of thread.

Step 16.7: Trim a point on one end of each of the two foam strips remaining from the body. Tie the pointed ends to the top/bottom of the clip. Strip the fuzzy material from the base of a brown hackle feather, and tie it to the back of the clip. Bind the stem to the clip while advancing the thread to its center.

Step 16.8: Wrap the hackle several turns, covering the back half of the clip. Tie it off, and trim the surplus. Pull the top foam over the wrapped hackle, and bind it in place. Repeat the process with the bottom strip. Trim off the waste end of each strip of foam, and cover-wrap over the trimmed ends.

Step 16.9: Tie on a second wing of clear Antron, and trim it even with the first. Use a fine-tooth comb to break apart the fibers if they tend to stick together. Tie on the eyes centered between the wing and the front loop using several criss-cross wraps. Tie several herls (peacock or brown ostrich) on the clip, then apply wraps both behind and in front of the eyes. Tie off the herls, and trim the waste ends. Personally I like to tie off and apply the whip-finish behind the eyes, but it is a choice the tier can easily make. Coat the whip-finish with head cement to complete the fly.

Chapter 17

Flex Sculpin

When we were getting ready to leave Missoula after establishing the flies for *LaFontaine Originals*, Volume III, I asked Gary if he had plans for any type of sculpin streamer. I hadn't seen any mention of this type of pattern in any of our preliminary work. He responded that he had several patterns with the field team and would let us know the results when they were available. We were discussing sculpins in general as we said our good-byes. I don't remember which one of us made the point (Gary, I think) that the fins were an important part of the pattern's attraction and should definitely be a prominent feature. We all agreed and went our separate ways, trusting Gary to let us know when he had a viable pattern.

That session had been fairly early in the summer, and as the season progressed I forgot about the fly—until one day a box showed up in the mail. The package didn't have a name on the return address, so I set it aside to review later, thinking it was probably fly patterns for a column Gretchen and I write for *Fly Fish America* magazine.

Several weeks later I received an e-mail from Gary, who wanted to know what I thought of the new Flex Sculpin he had sent. I was dumbstruck. I didn't remember seeing a box arrive from him and had no idea where it might be. Sometimes we would receive as many as a dozen flies a month for the magazine, and I had forgotten about the box from Missoula. A couple of panic-stricken hours later, I found the box from Gary. The fly looked super, and I especially appreciated the very prominent fins we all had agreed were an important feature. I e-mailed him back, advising that the pattern looked great and asking if he could share any of the field team's test results. The e-mail I received back a couple of days later included a lot more information than I really needed, and the following quote I'm providing in the next paragraph.

Gary wrote, "Sculpins are slimy creatures. They have a lot of wiggle to them. That's why we chose a flex hook for the design of this fly. The whole pattern has the shape and color of the sculpin, and it comes alive in the water. Fish it with a slow, almost dead-drift retrieve right along the bottom. Really bounce it along the tops of the rocks."

I couldn't have agreed with Gary more about the "really bounce it along the tops of the rock" statement. My personal experience fishing sculpin patterns had proved they needed to be near or at the bottom. We tied about a dozen of the new fly for our own fly boxes, knowing we would soon be traveling to Idaho to visit relatives and expected to spend some time on one of central Idaho's great cutthroat fisheries. It was to be a twofold trip—visiting relatives for Gretchen and fishing for me.

The travel day finally arrived, and ten long hours later we were visiting relatives in Boise. We visited here and visited there and visited and visited and visited... until I started to wonder if I'd ever see any water. Finally we arrived at the Lochsa River. As we were rigging up our rods, Gretchen asked me, "What [pattern] are you starting out with?" "Gary's Flex Sculpin," I responded. "Yeah, me too," she advised as she headed for the river. She doesn't often beat me to the water, but she sure did this time.

When I got to the river, the first thing I saw was her rod bent in an arch. *Wow, she's already got one,* I thought as I headed downstream to start fishing. I had made several casts, kind of dead-drifting the fly like Gary suggested, when I saw the end of my fly line twitch and set the hook into something real solid. It didn't take me long to realize I had a rockfish...snag...the bottom...whatever you want to call it, but I'm certainly not going to print here what was going through my mind. I tried my usual bag of tricks to free the hook, including attempting to roll-cast the fly off the offending rock, but had to finally give up, break it off, and tie on another. Two flies later I finally did hang into a really nice fish that promptly wrapped me around a submerged obstruction that I ended up breaking off as well. My day wasn't going so well. Half of my Flex Sculpins were gone, I didn't have a fish to hand for my effort, and I had driven a thousand miles to get to this point in time, on this river, etc.

An hour later I was headed upstream to find Gretchen to see if I can "beg, borrow, or steal" a Flex Sculpin from her. I ran into her headed in my direction. As we sat on a large rock side by side, we compared almost identical stories—several good-size fish lost and a dozen Flex Sculpins anchored securely to the bottom of the river.

We headed for the truck to tie a few more flies on the tailgate using our travel tying kit. We elected to leave some of the lead out of the body, making it lighter than Gary had suggested. The new flies didn't hang up on the bottom, but they didn't prove very attractive to the fish either. Gary was right on; the flies really needed to be on or near the bottom. The heavily weighted patterns hung up more often than we would have liked, but they also produced fish—a lot of fish. The lighter flies didn't snag as often, but they produced fewer fish. We didn't get skunked, but we came awful close.

Back at the drawing board (the tailgate of the truck), we designed flies into the wee hours by lantern light. Gretchen suggested we try tying the flies so that the hook point would ride up, making the pattern less prone to snag the bottom. We tried several ways of weighting the hook/clip, and found the point-up idea worked best when the lead wire was anchored along the top of the shank and then double-wrapped from there. The extra weight of the lead strand placed on top of the shank along with the placement of the materials caused the fly to travel in the water column with its point up.

We determined the new (and revised) pattern a success the next day on the water. We only lost a couple of flies the whole day, rather than that many an hour the previous afternoon. Oh, yeah! It also produced a lot of fish. I do have to admit the second day we switched to heavier-weight rods to "horse" some of the fish away from submerged structure that had cost us several flies and fish the day before.

Today I'm tying the pattern as Gary designed it; but at Step 4, where he added the lead wire, I'm also illustrating how we modified the fly so that the hook would ride point up. You can decide what method works best for you and your water conditions, then adjust your patterns accordingly. Whichever you decide, I don't think you'll be disappointed in how the fish respond to this great new pattern.

Flex Sculpin

Rear Section

Hook: Size 4 to 8, ringed eye

Thread: Brown

Tail: Pheasant tail fibers

Rib: Copper wire

Back: Pleasant tail fibers over brown Antron yarn

Weight: Lead wire, double layer (or more)

Body: White marabou, wrapped

Pectoral fins: Grouse or Hungarian partridge feathers

Front Section

Clip: Flex Clip to match hook size

Wing/collar: Brown dyed deer hair

Head: Brown dyed deer hair, spun and trimmed

Step 17.1: Mount the hook in the vise, and apply a thread base that starts one-third of the shank back from the eye. Wrap to the end of the shank and back to the starting point. Select a clump of pheasant tail fibers, and tie them to the hook to form a tail about as long as the span of the gape. Select a section of copper wire, and tie it to the back of the hook to later use as a rib. Trim off the waste materials.

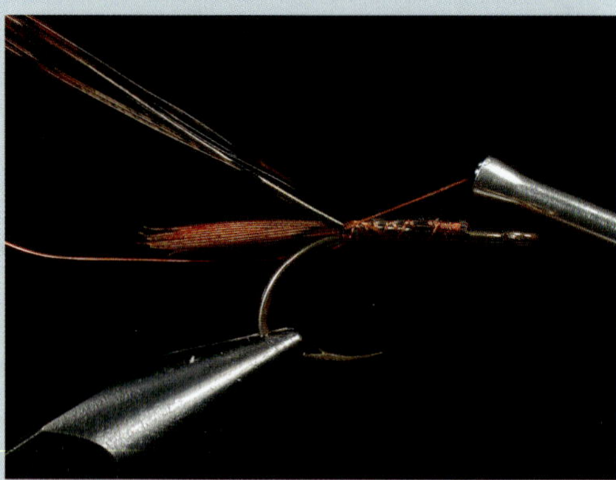

Step 17.2: Select another clump of pheasant tail fibers, and tie them to the hook so that they stick out the back. Make sure they are longer than the tail so that the two don't get tangled together. I like to take a single wrap of thread around this clump of pheasant tail fibers to further ensure they don't become mixed with the tail. Trim any waste fibers.

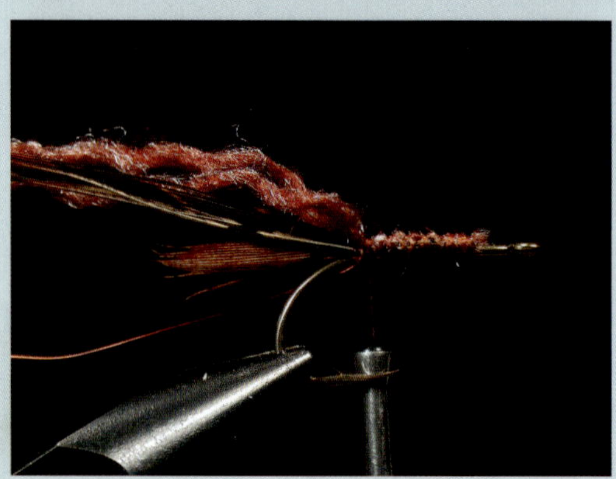

Step 17.3: Cut a 4-inch segment of four-strand brown Antron yarn, and separate out two of the pieces. Tie them to the hook directly on top of the fibers from the last step. Notice that I left the thread at the back of the hook in preparation for the next part of the process.

Step 17.4: Starting at the back of the hook, wrap a double layer of lead (or nonlead) wire. Trim off any tag ends, then wrap over the wire using open thread wraps. The wide wraps anchor the lead in place without slipping between each turn of the wire. A drop of glue is a good idea, if you wish. I am holding another hook constructed up to this same step. It's prepared to posture itself in the reverse position in the water column. I've run the extra strand of lead wire along the hook hank to overbalance the hook, causing the finished fly to flip over in the water. If I were completing an upside-down Flex Sculpin—I'm not, so don't get confused—I'd trim off the wire sticking out from the hook before advancing to the next step.)

Step 17.5: Select a full white marabou plume, and strip away any of the fibers that don't reach all the way to the tip of the feather. Tie the tips to the hook shank, bundle the feather with the thread, and wrap them (rope style) forward to the front of the hook. Tie off the feather, and trim the waste to finish the underbody.

Step 17.6: Pull the brown yarn over the wrapped marabou, and bind it to the front of the shank. Repeat the process with the pheasant tail fibers. Trim off the waste from both materials. Wrap the copper wire forward to form the rib. Tie it off, and trim the surplus.

Step 17.7: Pluck two grouse (or partridge) feathers from the skin, and strip the fuzzy material from the base of the stems. Tie them to the sides of the hook to form the pectoral fins. Trim off the waste part of the feathers, and apply a whip-finish to complete the rear section of the fly.

Step 17.8: Take the hook out of the vise, and attach a Flex Clip. Place it in the vise with the hook positioned behind the clip and the point nestled in the jaws slot for safety reasons. Attach the brown tying thread to the front of the clip, and close the loop using several thread wraps. Apply a whip-finish, and trim the thread from the clip. Attach single-strand floss (I used black or color of choice) at the back of the clip, closing that loop as well. Trim off the tag end. Select, clean, and stack a clump of brown dyed deer hair. Remove it from the stacker, measure it for length (even with the ends of the fins), and trim off the excess. Tie it to the clip to form a half collar/wing. Advance the floss in front of that application in preparation for the next step.

Step 17.9: Select a clump of dyed deer hair, remove the underfur, and spin it around the clip. Repeat the process a second time and even a third if it is needed to fill in the area between the two loops on the clip. Whip-finish, and trim the floss from the clip.

Step 17.10: Turn the clip/hook assembly over in the vise jaws, or rotate the jaws one-half turn, depending on the type of vise you are using. Cut the hair off the bottom of the clip close/parallel to it. Be careful at the back of the clip, because the part of the loop that points away from it can really mess up a pair of scissors if you get too close to it during the trimming process.

Step 17.11: Trim the top of the head, angling upward from the front loop of the clip. Be careful: Don't accidentally cut off the wing/collar.

Step 17.12: Trim each side by slanting the scissors outward from the front loop of the clip. Again be careful: It's real easy to accidentally cut the wrong hair. I like to use the rotating feature of my vise to place the fly in a position to more easily reach each part I want to trim. One useful modification—besides the upside-down concept—is to replace the deer hair wing/collar with one constructed from dyed brown marabou. If you try this idea, be sure to tie it short so it won't tend to foul around the hook/fins.

Chapter 18

Floating Flex Crayfish

*T*here I was in the front of our driftboat giggling like a little kid. Why? Well, let me give you a little background. We were on the lower Madison River near Bozeman, Gretchen was rowing the boat, and I was playing a really nice brown trout that fell for one of Gary's floating crayfish patterns we had tied with him the previous day.

Again you ask yourself, *Why is Al so happy?* Think about it! I'm the one playing the fish with my *wife* on the oars. There are not many guys lucky enough to have a wife who rows a driftboat as well as many guides and, more important, loves doing it! Besides, the fish was bigger than most for that section of water, and I had taken it on a floating fly, well almost.

Right now any of you reading these words who have spent time on that piece of water are about to call me a "fabricator of words," or something worse! I know—I couldn't believe what was happening either. I had guided that stretch of river for several years and caught a lot of fish on crayfish patterns, but all of them were heavily weighted monstrosities. We usually presented them deep in the bare areas between the weed beds using a strike indicator. The down-and-dirty system was deadly on the resident brown trout.

I had never even considered using a surface crayfish until Gary told me about his new pattern and technique on the phone several weeks earlier. As he detailed the wonders of this fly, I had started to get the "itch" to visit him in Missoula so that we could script a few more patterns, including the Floating Flex Crayfish. When I got off the phone, Gretchen accused me of just wanting to see Gary again (and she was probably right). But when I explained to her what Gary had said about the new crayfish pattern and technique, she was the one who suggested taking the driftboat "just in case we needed it." I didn't put up much of an argument; I was on my way out the door to hook the boat to the truck.

Several days later, as we were winding up our meeting with Gary, he asked if we were staying in town for dinner that night. Gretchen told him we couldn't because we still wanted to get to Bozeman that evening. What she didn't tell him was that our ultimate goal happened to be a fishing access on the lower Madison River (just outside Bozeman), where we planned to spend the night sleeping in the back of the truck. Why? So we could get an early start on the river the next day.

Early the next morning we rigged our rods to present the fly as Gary had suggested by using the "Yo-Yo Technique" he had developed for fishing floating patterns subsurface. For those of you not familiar with this method, it may sound like an oxymoron (and it was new to us on that day several years ago). The angler places a buoyant, floating fly on a short leader (3 or 4 feet at the most) and ties it to a full sink line. When cast into the water, the line sinks quickly to the bottom, pulling the floating fly with it. After the line comes to rest on the bottom with the fly suspended above it, the angler starts the retrieve. Each strip part of the retrieve pulls the fly lower in the water column, but the pattern's buoyancy causes it to rise when the angler pauses. The strip/pause retrieve causes the fly to dip and dive (yo-yo) in the water; it drives fish crazy when presented under the right conditions.

My concern that day was the moving water in the Madison. I felt some of it was too fast to present the fly with a full sink line, so we prepared two rods. The first, rigged exactly as Gary suggested, we planned to use in the real slow backwater sloughs often encountered in that stretch of river. I rigged the second rod with a floating line, long leader, split shot, and a strike indicator to use in the faster water around the weed beds where the big brown trout lived. I had to adjust the distance between the split shot and the fly until the two were in concert with each other and the water conditions. That day 3 feet seemed to be the right space between the two, but that distance can vary based on water speed and depth. We caught most of our fish on the split-shot rig, but the big boy that made me so happy fell for the fly presented with a full-sink line in a backwater slough. Darn, just thinking about ole brownie makes me smile again.

Let's fast-forward to present day, summer 2007. I just returned from a quick trip to the Snake River south of our home in Boise, Idaho, where I escaped from work for a short time. There the smallmouth bass are usually suckers for a heavily weighted crayfish pattern presented deep in the water column under a strike indicator. Today the fishing was a bit slow until I tied on a Floating Flex Crayfish using the split-shot method. That pattern seemed to be the common denominator to success today. I've tested the same fly several times in the past on the Snake with minimal success, but today it triggered something in those bass that was amazing. Will it happen next time I visit my ole buddy the Snake River? I don't know, but I guarantee I'll have several Floating Flex Crayfish patterns in my fly box, including the one we're going to tie together.

Also, if you haven't done so, give the Yo-Yo Technique a try. You might be pleasantly surprised—it can be deadly.

Floating Flex Crayfish

Rear Section

Hook: Size 4 to 8, ringed eye

Thread: Brown

Tail: Pheasant tail fibers

Rib: Brown thread

Back: Pheasant tail fibers

Underbody: Edgewater foam cylinder or wrapped strip of foam

Overbody: Brown Antron dubbing or yarn

Front Section

Clip: Flex Clip to match hook size

Foam: Brown strip, top and bottom

Pincers: Pheasant tail fibers

Step 18.1: Place the hook in the vise, attach the tying thread a short distance back from the eye, and wrap to the end of the hook shank. Leave a long tag of thread to use later as a rib. Select a clump of pheasant tail fibers, and tie them to the hook to form a tail shorter than the span of the hook gape. Select a second clump of pheasant tail fibers, and tie them to the hook by their tips with the butt ends pointing to the rear. Make sure those fibers are longer than the tail. Trim off all waste. Leave the thread hanging at the back of the hook. (When I stripped the second clump of fibers from the stem, the curled ends kept them in a bundle well separated from the tail.)

Step 18.2: Here you can use an Edgewater (or Rainey's) foam cylinder or a strip of closed-cell foam. All I had in my stock was a white foam cylinder, so I elected to wrap a narrow brown strip for the underbody. I cut this strip so that it was as wide as half the hook gape, then trimmed a point on one end. I tied the pointed end on the hook, then wrapped the underbody, tied it off, and trimmed the waste. I recommend placing an application of superglue before wrapping the foam, but that is a personal choice. I finished this step by placing a snug (not tight) crisscross wrap over the foam underbody.

Step 18.3: I have better luck wrapping a strand of yarn over the bulky foam rather than using dubbing, so I have applied the overpart of the body using that material. Brown Antron touch dubbing is also a good choice. In either case, make sure the thread is hanging at the front of the hook.

Step 18.4: Pull the second bundle of pheasant tail fibers over the body, and anchor them in place. Trim off the waste fibers. Wrap the tag of thread forward over the body, and tie it off to complete the rib. Trim off excess rib thread.

Step 18.5: Whip-finish and trim the tying thread from the hook. Remove it from the vise, slip a Flex Clip through the eye, and position the clip in the jaws. Attach the thread to the front of the clip, place several wraps to close the front loop, and trim off the tag end of the thread. Wrap to the back of the clip, and close that eye as well. Leave the thread hanging at the back of the clip in preparation for the next step.

Step 18.6: Cut a 6-inch strip of foam about as wide as the hook gape. Clip it in half, then trim a point on one end of each piece. Tie the pointed ends to the top and bottom of the clip. Wrap the thread almost all of the way forward to the front loop, stopping just short of it.

Step 18.7: Select a clump of pheasant tail fibers, and tie them to the offside of the clip with the tips pointing forward. They should be as long as the complete clip. Repeat the process on the nearside. Leave the thread at the front of the clip, trim all waste fibers, and push the pheasant clumps back so that they stick out straight.

Step 18.8: Pull the bottom strip of foam forward and anchor it in place. Repeat the process with the top strip of foam. Trim off both, whip-finish, and cut the thread from the clip.

Step 18.9: Place a drop of head cement to complete the fly. (I know this doesn't look much like a crayfish, but don't knock it until you've tried it. Those of you who are Gary's fans should know by now that many of his patterns don't look the same to us as they do to the fish, who are the real critics.)

Chapter 19

Fluttering Stone

ary's comments taken from a tape dated August 2001: "This great fly pattern was developed by Nevin Stephenson, my guiding partner during my years on the Big Hole River. We realized that we needed two types of stoneflies: one that was low-riding, flush in the surface (like the Flex Stone), and one that was high-riding (like the Fluttering Stone or EZ2C Stonefly) on its hackle tips. There were already a number of good low-riding stonefly imitations for the giant salmonfly and the golden stonefly, but we felt like we needed a better high-riding imitation. Nevin came up with the Fluttering Stone, and it was an instant success. The way we fished the fly was with a drift-and-twitch sequence."

Gary went on to explain a bit more about the body of this fly, telling all of us the first couple of test flies didn't have the poly yarn combed out; it tended to tangle around the hook bend/shank. After he and Nevin stumbled on the idea of combing out the poly material, the problem was solved. The result was this great high-floating pattern.

I'd like to digress a moment. After listening to the tape of our scripting session, I remembered that day had been a really special one for Gary. Somehow the "word" had gotten out that we were in town working with him, and well-recognized people in the fly-fishing industry just started showing up at the motel we were using as a work location. People from nearby states like Oregon and Washington drove over to say hello. Rhea Topping, a well-recognized casting instructor from the eastern part of our country, learned about our meeting while driving down Interstate 90 and stopped to visit (and enjoy pizza for lunch). For a while the motel room got real small as "friends" showed up to wish Gary (and the rest of us) well. I recorded *all* the conversations, which at times sounded more like pandemonium.

I always recorded our sessions using a video camera (focused on a stationary vise for the times we actually tied a fly) and capturing the sound by placing microphones around the room, on Gary, and on whoever was the selected tier (usually Paul Stimpson). By doing so, I was able to later isolate different conversations that had all transpired simultaneously. As I checked the different soundtracks, I picked up Gary talking about designing flies and being the modest person he always was: "I don't think I ever developed much of anything. I just threw out ideas to a group of people, captured the best suggestion, and incorporated them into the pattern. Like the House Fly we worked out this morning; Paul figured out the body, and Gretchen solved the wing problem. Or the Fluttering Stone that Nevin developed and I helped with the body. Most of the flies in *The Dry Fly* were developed [assembled] that way."

It was fun to check some of the other channels while quietly eavesdropping on the conversations around the room. "That rainbow jumped three times before it came off...sales are up a bit after a really flat year...the caddis were so thick they were crawling up my nose...I'm headed to South America next month to teach several classes and fish with..." Those conversations went on for several hours, ebbing and flowing as people joined us, left, and others took their place. Paul finally did get the Fluttering Stone tied so that we knew how Gary wanted it to appear on tape, but it took most of the day. I'm not complaining, mind you; it was one of the more memorable times Gretchen and I, with Paul and Char, had ever spent with Gary. What's amazing, the whole day was totally unplanned. But I've digressed enough while traveling down memory lane—let's get back to the pattern at hand.

I have to admit the fly surprised me a bit when we finally got it tied. Quite frankly, it was a bit like several other patterns I had used in past years. One of the similar flies was developed by our friend Lee Clark (Clark's Stonefly) and only differed from Nevin's pattern by the lack of antennae. I tied a pattern in the 1980s that was identical, except that mine had a furled body while Nevin's was combed. My point here is one Gretchen and I often make about "developed, new flies." It's amazing the similarities that surface when fly tiers who do not know one another assemble flies intended to mimic the same critter. On the other hand, every now and again someone like Gary LaFontaine comes along who really thinks "outside the box" and develops some really amazing patterns.

I guess that's what *LaFontaine's Legacy* is really all about, different ideas that will spark a creative synergy in all of you. Writing it (and listening to the hours of tape) has certainly energized me—*and* the book isn't done yet! Let me get back to work and tie this pattern before I really get off on a tangent.

Fluttering Stone

Hook: Size 2 to 16, 2 or 3x long dry fly

Thread: Orange

Body: Orange polypropylene yarn, extended and combed

Wing: Dark deer or elk hair, stacked

Antenna: Brown monofilament

Hackle: Brown

This is a pattern that you definitely want in your fly box almost any time during the year. Gary suggested using it when the adult stoneflies are "skittering" across the water's surface, and we certainly concur. Note that we've used a different method of hackling a fly that you might want to try.

This pattern is equally effective in a range of sizes and colors. Just change the materials to imitate a wide range of natural stonefly or caddisfly adults.

Step 19.1: Set the hook in the vise, and apply a thread base that covers the back half of the shank. Trim the waste end, then leave the bobbin hanging in the center of the hook.

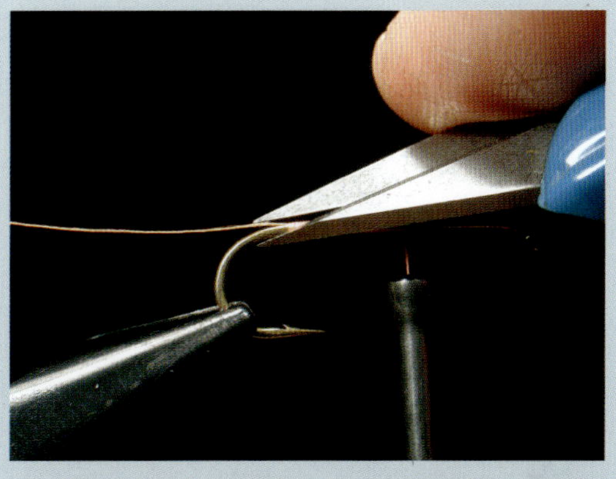

Step 19.2: Cut two short pieces of poly yarn from the skein, and tie them to the center of the hook with most of their bulk pointing to the rear of shank. Trim the waste ends (pointing forward) at a severe angle, then wrap over that part to start a tapered hackle platform that I'll complete in the next step. Cut off the part pointing to the rear so that it is equal in length to the hook shank. Use a fine-tooth comb to fluff and untangle the fibers.

Step 19.3: Select a clump of dark deer or elk hair, clean out the underfur, and even the tips in a stacker. The best hair for wings is located on the animal along the backbone, over the shoulder, and down the rump. That hair tends to be dark gray in color near the base of the fiber where it joins the hide. Tie the wing on the hook using several tight thread wraps, then cut the waste ends at a severe angle. Cover-wrap over them, leaving the thread hanging near the hook eye. (Gary almost never stacked the hair on his wings. He acquiesced when Paul and I argued that an unstacked wing "just didn't look good on a commercial fly." The friendly "unstacked wing" argument went on for several years. Most of the time it was the four of us against one, but Gary usually wouldn't give in. He did this time; I guess we caught him at a weak moment.)

Step 19.4: Clip a piece of brown monofilament (I'm using six-pound Maxima) from the spool, then cut it in half. Tie one piece on the offside of the hook, with most of it pointing forward. Repeat the process on the nearside. If you position the pieces correctly, the natural curve will slope outward on each side of the shank. Trim them both so that they are the same length. Take a couple of wraps of thread in front of the new antenna, then leave it hanging behind them.

Step 19.5: Gary wanted this fly heavily hackled and suggested using two feathers. Please do so if you have them, or you can accomplish the same thing using one long saddle, as I'm doing. First strip the fuzzy material from the base of the stem, and tie the feather to the hook close to the eye. Wrap the hackle back to meet the wing fibers, leaving small spaces between each turn of the feather.

Step 19.6: Wrap the rest of the hackle forward, filling in the spaces remaining from the previous step. Tie off the feather, and trim it from the hook. A whip-finish and a drop of head cement are all that's needed to complete the fly.

Chapter 20

House Fly

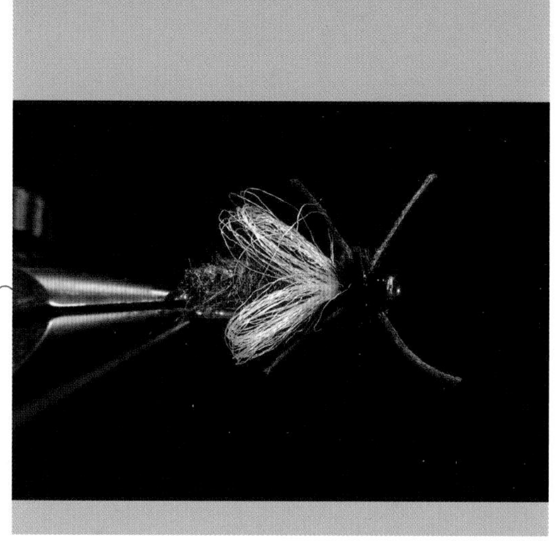

One of the things Gary wanted to accomplish was to have a fly for every possible fishing situation. One day he called Paul saying, "We've got to have a housefly." Paul made the mistake of questioning Gary by saying, "The housefly is not aquatic." Gary patiently explained that fish don't just eat aquatic insects, as evidenced by the importance of grasshoppers, beetles, and other terrestrial insects as a food source. "But, houseflies?" questioned Paul even further.

Gary told him to try an experiment. Set a large pan of water outside overnight and see what's in it in the morning. Gary assured him that there would always be several common houseflies in the mix of terrestrial insects. After Paul ran the test, he had to agree with Gary, and the two set out to design a fly to fit the need.

About this time in the process, Paul called us. Gretchen answered the phone, and after the usual greetings Paul got down to business. What did we think a good body would be for a housefly? We didn't have a clue but agreed to run the "water pan" experiment in our backyard and get back with him after we had caught some flies. In the meantime Paul and Char were chasing houseflies around their home, trying to capture a couple to study live. Paul seemed to think imitating a live insect was more important than one that had drowned in a pan of water. He was right, because some of the hairy fibers on their body seemed to disappear after a night in the water. At least that's how it looked when we used our magnifying glass to study the wet critters we captured.

In time we agreed that peacock herl applied Double Magic style using Antron touch dubbing sounded like a good option to us, but when Gary viewed the results, he said the bodies had too much sparkle and sent us back to the drawing board. We tried reducing the amount of touch dubbing and got another refusal. Darn! This was almost like presenting a fly to a difficult spring-creek trout. Gary wasn't buying what we had to offer. One of us finally suggested using a standard black synthetic dubbing in place of the Antron touch dubbing but applying it Double Magic style. That's what Gary was looking for; he rose to it on the first presentation. He later explained to us he was looking for fine hairs around the body rather than highlights the Antron produced. He was happy up to this point.

When we tied the fly on camera for him, the wing just didn't look right. Paul would put on a clump of Antron fibers and trim them to a rounded shape. Gary would look at them and again send us back to the drawing board. We discussed (and tried) several different ideas. Less Antron but trimmed differently? No! We even tried tying the bundles of Antron "spent style," and still Gary did not like the way the fly looked. Finally Gretchen suggested double, looped wings—that was the answer. Gary loved the look of the fly. We recorded the information and later included the House Fly on *LaFontaine Originals,* Volume V.

After all the flies we filmed for Gary, I have to admit there were two or three I never did try; the House Fly was one. When Gretchen and I were working on this chapter of the book, I decided I should at least give the pattern a quick test to prove to myself it would fool a fish. Paul and Char were already converts.

Often in the evening Gretchen and I will enjoy a cup of coffee or a glass of iced tea while sitting next to our pond. Listening to the water run over the rocks and watching the koi eat their dinner had a therapeutic, calming effect on us both. The pressures of the day would melt away as we sat there and talked with the babbling water as a background.

Ideas also came to mind under the same circumstances. I'm thinking, *I need to test the House Fly. Why travel all the way to the river. I have fish right here. Hum.* I also was very aware Gretchen protected "her fish" with a vengeance. I had decided that I'd better leave them alone, when all of a sudden she decided to go to the store a couple of miles away to pick up something she forgot on her way home from work.

When I saw her pull out of the driveway, I grabbed the "miniature fly rod" I often use to make "joke" photographs of a small fish so that it would look bigger when placed beside the rod. I tied on a small House Fly, made my presentation, and Big Boy (Gretchen's prize koi) nailed it almost as soon as it hit the water. He would have run me into my backing except that the pond was too small to allow that, but I certainly had a fight on my hands anyway.

I just about had that darned fish worn down to the point where I could release it when Gretchen walked in looking for the checkbook she forgot and caught me in the act. Darn! To make a long story short, I made her "list" big time, and it was less than good for me!

Regarding the pattern, I had to rate the fly a success (at least Big Boy loved it), but I figured any additional testing should be done somewhere farther from home and retired the fly to a slot in the terrestrial box. If any of you have a koi pond in your yard, I recommend you test the House Fly somewhere *away* from the home— your life will be much less complicated than mine is right now. Of course by the time you read these words, things should be better at my home. I hope!

House Fly

Hook: Size 14 to 18, 1x long standard dry fly

Thread: Black

Underbody: Black foam, strip or cylinder

Body: Peacock herl and black dubbing, Double Magic style

Wing: Clear Antron, looped and separated

Legs: Black Kevlar thread or fine rubber leg material

Head: Black ostrich herl

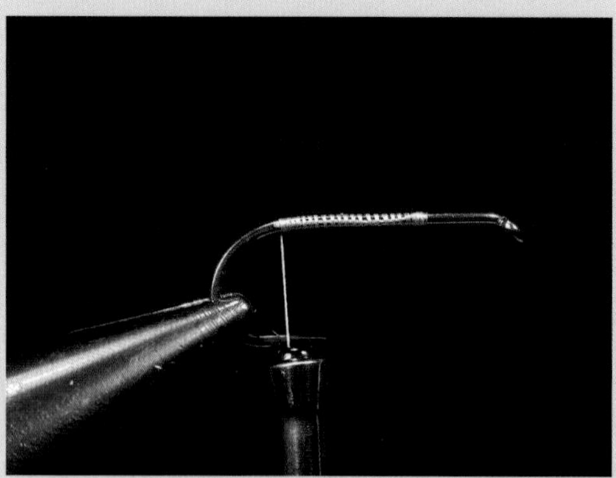

Step 20.1: Select a hook, place it in the vise, and cover the back two-thirds of the shank with a thread base. Leave it hanging at the back of the hook. (I've used gray thread, foam, and dubbing in the first three steps so that it will show against the black background, but be sure to use black materials on your pattern. I didn't use a different color of peacock or ostrich herl because they seemed to have enough highlights to show well in the photograph.)

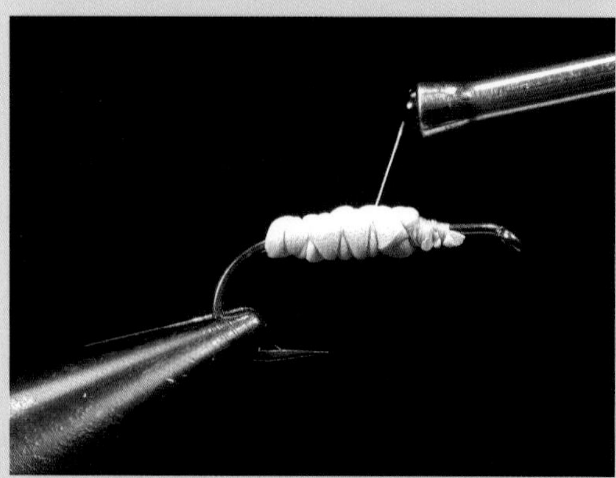

Step 20.2: Cut a strip of foam smaller in width than the hook gape, and clip a point on one end. Tie this end to the back of the hook while advancing the thread to the one-third position. Wrap the foam forward to meet the thread, tie it off, and trim the surplus. Wrap back over the foam, then forward using snug, not tight thread turns. Many tiers like to use a layer of superglue when they wrap a foam body, do so if you wish. Or slip a section of round foam on the hook and glue it into position; the choice is yours.

Step 20.3: Select several peacock herls, and tie them to the top of the foam underbody by their tips while wrapping to the back of the hook, then trim as needed. Pull the thread into a dubbing loop, place Super Tacky Wax on it, and touch (standard) black dubbing to it. Do not twist the dubbing material around the thread. Secure the peacock herl in the dubbing loop, and spin the tool to twist the two materials (dubbing and herl) into chenille. Wrap the newly formed material over the foam, tie it off, and trim the waste to complete the body.

Step 20.4: Select a strand of clear Antron yarn, form it into a loop, and tie it to the hook to form a flat, Trude-style wing that is no longer than the end of the body. Use a bodkin to separate the loop into two wings.

Step 20.5: Clip two sections of Kevlar thread (or other fairly stiff thread) from the spool, and tie them to the hook to form four legs directly in front of the wings. Pull the legs all up together, and trim them to length, about three-fourths of the length of the body.

Step 20.6: Tie one black ostrich herl on the shank behind the legs, then finish binding it to the hook while wrapping the thread forward to meet the eye. Wind the herl forward, making sure to figure-eight wrap it around the legs before finishing the head in front of them. Tie it off, and trim the waste. A whip-finish and a drop of head cement complete the fly.

Chapter 21

Lady Heather Double Wing

*S*everal years ago Gary called Paul asking if he could tie several sets of Double Wings for the Book Mailer. He wanted to offer a "special deal" to a few customers: a box with twelve dozen flies in it—four each of sizes 12, 14, and 16 in a dozen colors. Gary had one little problem; he only had eleven Double Wing colors in the catalog. Paul suggested they design another Double Wing while Gary looked over the color combinations he offered in the Book Mailer. The two decided they could definitely use a fly that fell in between a cream and a gray Double Wing.

While on the telephone, the two brainstormed/developed the parts of the fly you see here today and named it the Lady Heather. After the field team finished testing the new fly, Gary decided to write an introduction for the special box of Double Wings explaining when and why to use them and ordered ten full sets of 144 flies each from Paul to "test market" the idea in the next copy of the Book Mailer.

The concept was so popular that for the next two years, Paul tied sets of Double Wings (almost full-time) until he had them coming out of his ears (almost!). He got really, really tired of tying them and finally cried "uncle." Gary had to retire the idea, his tier (Paul) had worn out on him. Maybe after this book is published, we might talk Paul into tying a few sets of Double Wings again!

Gretchen and I especially want to thank Cathy Ransier and Marcy Chovanak, current owners of the Book Mailer, for making Gary's short article "The Magic of the Double Wing" available for our use here. Their permission allows me to bring a bit of Gary to all of you. Enjoy!

The Magic of the Double Wing

Gary LaFontaine

There is a formula for attractor dry flies, and it applies not only to Double Wings but also to Wulffs, Trudes, Humpies, Stimulators, or any style of attractor that comes in a series of colors. The formula is deceptively simple, but it will increase the catch rate for attractors by 20 to 30 percent. Here is the formula—match the main color of the attractor dry fly to the color of the prevalent light.

Why does this magic formula work so well? Get in the car and drive around sometime at dusk. Really look at things when the light is intensely orange. Pick out things that are "warm" colors—things that are red and orange. Look how they look like they are on fire. It's because they are the same color as the prevalent light. They are absorbing all of those orange light waves and bouncing them back. And the same thing happens with every other color. Green things will bounce back green light waves, and yellow things will bounce back yellow light waves. So all you need to do is follow the formula to have an intensely bright fly.

Look, look, look! Look at the light around you. Really look at it. It's different at different times of the day. It's different in different places. To know how to pick the intensely bright fly, you have to really look at the light. Let me give you a few examples. In the evening the light is that reddish-orange color, so pick a reddish-orange fly. If you are fishing around a lot of vegetation, the green leaves reflect a lot of green light and you need to fish with a greenish fly. During the middle of the day, sunlight tends to be yellowish-green and a bright yellow fly is the right choice.

That intensely bright fly—the right color in the right light—is a strong attractor when it's floating on the surface. Fish see the hazy aura of color just fine any time of the day when they are laying on the bottom of the stream looking up at the top of the water, and there is something about the oddly bright pattern that triggers the curiosity of a fish. He just has to come up and smack that fly. So in general the right color fly is better than the wrong color fly when it comes to dry fly attractors.

Why is the Double Wing better than other dry fly attractors? It is specifically designed with a hot spot of color at the back of the body. There is a stub tail of Antron yarn (of the right color). On top of this stub tail there are two wings, one to form a contrasting background and the other to form a white reflector to catch all stray light rays bouncing up from the water. Every tying step around the back portion of the fly is meant to accentuate the color of the sparkling Antron yarn. On the Double Wing, color isn't used randomly.

The Double Wings are a series of 12 patterns designed to meet every light condition the angler is going to encounter around the trout stream. Here are the 12 patterns and the conditions they are meant for:

1. Lime Double Wing—An excellent pattern around vegetation—plants reflect a lot of green light.
2. Orange Double Wing—For dusk when there is a magnificent reddish-orange sunset.
3. Royal Double Wing—The ultimate attractor—contains green, red, and brown highlights and works on riffles during midday as an all-around searching/attractor.

4. Yellow Double Wing—Midday attractor—also valuable as an imitation of certain yellow stoneflies (especially the #16 Yellow Sallies and the #8 Golden Stones).

5. Gray Double Wing—The oldest maxim is "gray day, gray fly." Use this pattern on dark overcast and rainy days.

6. Midnight Double Wing—A black fly for night fishing. The silhouette shows up against the sky.

7. Charm Double Wing—This is the pattern for the last moments of dusk after the sun sets, when the light tends to take on a bluish quality.

8. Pink Lady Double Wing—Pink for when the light is pink—late mornings and late afternoons.

9. White Double Wing—This is also a good fly for late, late evenings, mainly because it reflects all available light and it makes a good imitation of a moth.

10. Brown Double Wing—This is the in-between fly—use this pattern right in between the afternoon and evening. It's the "warm" fly, but not super warm.

11. Lady Heather Double Wing—This is a great, great attractor for those days that photographers call "cloudy bright." Clouds cover everything, but there is enough light coming through so that everything isn't a dark gray. Use the Lady Heather on these days. [Author's note: Gretchen and I have also found this pattern very effective in a couple of "tight" canyons we like to fish where the light is not directly on the stream except for a very short timeline during some parts of the day.]

12. Cream Double Wing—Another fine moth imitation; also one of my favorite very early morning patterns. Use this fly at dawn.

The key to using this series of Double Wings intelligently is using them at the right time. Trout aren't always ready to come up for dry flies. Sometimes they are plastered on the bottom and won't feed on anything except for nymphs (and sometimes they won't even take nymphs). But other times they may not be rising wildly, but they still may be willing to rise freely to the surface. They are just in a freewheeling mood. And this is when you want to try attractor dry flies.

When does this magic freewheeling period happen? I like to think of it in terms of hunger. Think of a pizza deliveryman. It's not going to be right after a heavy hatch—then the trout have already eaten and they are sitting on the bottom. The best time for attractors always seems to be a few hours before the hatch. It's like the trout are waiting for the pizza deliveryman. They are looking up at the surface expectantly—and they are willing to rush up and smack a strange looking bug floating along on top. That's the best time to use attractors.

Take your Double Wing selection out to the water. Look, really look, at the prevalent light. Try to match the hook size to the lip size of the fish present in the stream—the bigger the fish, the bigger the fly choice. And then if nothing is hatching, or if there is a sporadic hatch with only the occasional rise, pick out the right Double Wing. Read the holding water, trying to put the fly into the spots where fish are going to be resting between feeding sprees—that means casting a little bit closer to cover. Hang on for some splashy and hard strikes.

Lady Heather Double Wing

Hook: Size 8 to 18, 1 or 2x long dry fly

Thread: Gray

Tail: Light gray Antron, combed

Tip: Gray floss

Rear wing: Light gray deer barred with a black, felt-tip pen

Body hackle: Grizzly, clipped top and bottom

Body: Cream Antron touch dubbing

Front wing: White calf tail

Hackle: Grizzly, dun mix

Head: Thread

Gary originally tied this fly on a 1x long dry fly hook. Quite frankly it is difficult to get all the materials on a hook that short. Therefore, Gretchen and I often tie it on a 2x long dry fly hook or a 3x long curved hook similar to a TMC 200R.

Gray materials were used in the illustrations rather than white as suggested in the recipe to help provide photographic clarity.

Step 21.1: Select a dry fly hook, and place it in the vise; I'm using a 2x long hook, but select what you have available. Start the thread base about one-third of the shank length back from the eye. Wrap to the end of the shank, select a segment of Antron yarn, and tie it to the hook to form a tail equal to the hook gape in length. Trim off the surplus yarn, then use a fine-tooth comb to fluff the fibers so that the tail will reflect more light. The thread should be hanging directly above the hook point.

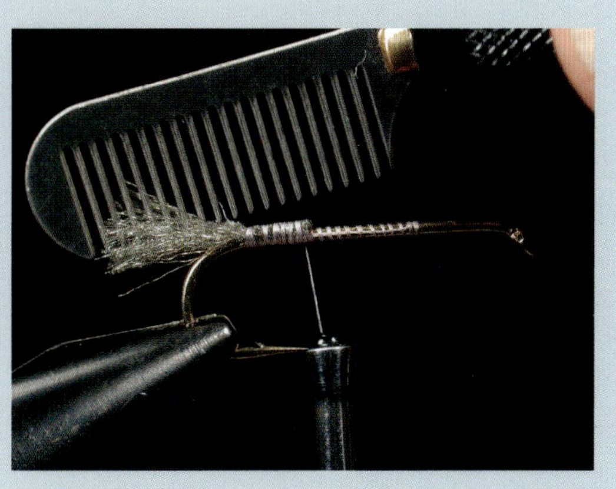

Step 21.2: Tie on a 6-inch piece of gray floss; wrap it back to meet the tail and then forward to the starting point. Tie it off, and trim the waste ends to complete the tip.

Step 21.3: Select, clean, and stack a clump of natural, gray deer hair. Tie it to the hook Trude style to form the first wing that is no longer than the tail. Trim off the waste fibers. (I like to bury the hair ends with thread wraps so that they help form a smooth underbody.)

Step 21.4: Pull the wing back, and use a felt-tip marker to place a couple of black bands across the compressed bundle. When I let go of the bundle of hair, the black bars cause the light filtering through the wing to have a "speckled" effect.

Step 21.5: Strip the fuzzy materials from the base of a grizzly feather, tie it to the back of the body (in front of the first wing), and leave it there for the moment. Apply dubbing wax to the thread, and pat a clump of touch dubbing to it. *Do not* twist the dubbing on the thread; instead wrap it forward to form the body. I like to stroke back the dubbing fibers after each turn of thread, but that is a personal choice.

Step 21.6: Palmer the hackle forward over the body, tie it off, and trim the surplus. Clip off the fibers from the bottom of the hook, then repeat the process on the top to complete the illusion of width.

Step 21.7: Select, clean, and stack a clump of calf tail hair. Tie it to the hook to form a second Trude-style wing whose tips are even with those in the first. Cut the waste fibers at a severe angle, and wrap thread over them, forming a tapered hackle platform. Leave the thread hanging directly in front of the second wing.

Step 21.8: Strip the fuzzy materials from the base of a grizzly and a dun hackle feather. Tie them to the hook in front of the second wing while advancing the thread to the eye. Trim off the waste ends of the stems. Wrap the grizzly hackle forward to meet the thread, tie it off, and trim away the excess. Make sure to leave spaces between each turn of feather so that the dun hackle will fit in the next step.

Step 21.9: Wind the dun feather forward, filling up the spaces prepared in the last step. At the front of the hook, tie it off and trim the extra. Apply a whip-finish, then follow it with a drop of head cement.

Chapter 22

Missouri River Sow Bug

W hat did Gary have on his mind?" Gretchen asked as I hung up the telephone. "He wanted us to send several items and gave some information about a pattern a member of his field team, Tony Perpignano, developed called the Missouri River Sow Bug," I answered as I started putting the items in a box to mail to him.

"So tell me about this fly," she prompted. I explained that it was based on another LaFontaine pattern, the Roll Over Scud, which was one of his "flies with motion" series. On the Roll Over Scud, Gary had placed lead wire on the top of the hook so that the fly would flip over in the water when the angler paused during his retrieve. On this fly, Tony had placed the wire on the side of the hook so that the pattern would wobble in the current, especially if it were under a bit of tippet tension caused by the angler.

"Sounds interesting," she said. "By the way, when are you taking me to the Missouri River like you've been promising for I don't know how long?" I looked around the office, and except for Gary's order we didn't have anything really pressing. "How about we leave this afternoon (a Thursday) and spend a long weekend on the section below Holter Dam in the Wolf Creek/Craig area? Do you want to stay in the motel at Wolf Creek or in the back of the truck?" Knowing what I had shared with her about the motel in question, she opted for the back of the truck. *Smart girl! That's why I married her,* I thought as I carried Gary's order to the street-side mailbox.

When I walked back into the house, she was already putting together food items for a several-day trip, so I headed for our workroom to tie a few flies for the trip. On the phone Gary had described Tony's fly as an off-weighted fly similar to an old Trueblood's Beaver Nymph comprising a short tail, a body/rib, and a beard hackle. It sounded really easy, so I tied a dozen for our trip. Darn! I liked the fly before ever using it, because it only took about twenty minutes to turn out that dozen. I was outside hooking up the driftboat to the truck in no time.

We were on the road long before lunchtime. Many hours later we arrived at the river a scant two hours before dark. There wasn't time to get the boat in the water and arrange a shuttle, so we put on our waders at the base of the large rock near camp, crossed the railroad tracks, and dropped down to the river.

We had to cross a slow-water side channel to get to the main body of the river. I reached out and grabbed Dubbin's (our fishing dog) collar and told Gretchen to wait just as she was about to step in the water. That side channel was alive with working fish, and several appeared to be large enough to measure in pounds rather than inches. We both stood in silence just watching the activity in front of us while the dog shivered with anticipation each time he heard another splash from a large fish breaking the waters surface.

The bank along the railroad tracks caused a bit of a backcasting problem, so we headed upstream about a hundred yards so that we could cross without spooking the fish. Even then we saw several large fish scoot for cover as we stepped into the placid water. On the other side of the channel, we stayed back from the water's edge as we headed back downstream to the working pod of fish.

Finally we were below them, deciding how to make our approach. I had tied on a fly developed by friend Bob Lay called the Missouri River Caddis before leaving the truck, while Gretchen had yet to attach anything to her leader. By default I was first to take a shot at the fish. Gretchen grabbed Dubbin's collar, while I got down on my hands and knees to make my final approach to the water's edge. First cast! Nothing. *Maybe there was a bit of drag on the fly,* I thought. The second cast included a perfect drift! My fly ended up downstream, totally ignored. After a dozen presentations I quietly backed away from the river to give Gretchen her chance.

"What fly were you using?" she asked when I joined her and Dubbin, who were hunkered down in the tall grass. "A Missouri River Caddis," I told her. She indicated that I hadn't had much luck with it and asked for one of Gary's new flies. With a Missouri River Sow Bug tied to her tippet, she crept up to the water a little farther upstream from the location I had inhabited.

Her first cast looked like a perfect dead-drift presentation, but the feeding fish totally ignored it. The same thing happened on her second and third casts. On the fourth cast she "ticked" a weed on her backcast, causing the line/leader to drop in the water at a bad angle to get a decent dead drift. She threw a short mend in the line to get it straight with the current and "bam"—she was into a really good trout that ran right up through the feeding pod of fish, sending them in every direction. She finally drew a big brown trout close to the bank so that I could net it for her. When the trout saw me coming in its direction with the net, it headed for open water, going right between the dog's legs. Dubbin had slipped into the middle of the action to "participate," and he yelped as the leader wrapped around his front leg and the trout jumped for the sky, but not loud enough to cover the sickening "snap" as the tippet and fish parted company. Oh, well, it had been fun for a while, and it was time to head for the truck if we wanted to arrive before total darkness made the trip more difficult.

During the next two and a half days, we had time to really test Tony's fly. We caught a lot of fish on it and found many of them responded to the "wiggle" it produced when a very, very slight amount of tension was placed on the leader. I'm not talking about stripping the fly, but rather a quick tug that often hits a pattern when mending to maintain a drag-free drift.

I know, most of you reading these pages don't end up tugging on your fly while mending your line, but for some reason it does happen to me once in a while. During this particular excursion, the fact I'm a lousy "mender" worked to my advantage.

On some subsequent trips, my poor mending skills worked against me, but not this time. I remember a time on the Bighorn River when... No, that's a story for another time. Instead I recommend all of you try this fly and draw you own conclusions. You may be pleasantly surprised like Gretchen and I were.

Missouri River Sow Bug

Hook: Size 12 to 20, scud
Thread: Brown
Weight: Two strips of lead wire (nonlead wire substitute)
Tail: Hen, grouse, or partridge fibers
Body: Gray muskrat dubbing, or color of choice
Rib: Tying thread
Hackle: Hen, grouse, or partridge fibers; beard style
Head: Thread

Step 22.1: Place the hook in the vise, and apply a thread base from the eye to a position directly above the hook barb. (On this style of hook it is difficult to identify the "end of the shank," so Gretchen and I have established the point directly above the hook barb as that position.) Wrap the thread forward almost all the way back (not quite) to the hook eye. Prepare two strips of lead wire, with one slightly longer than the other as illustrated.

Step 22.2: Tie the lead to the offside of the hook, binding one on top of the other. Trim them at an angle so that the bottom strip is a bit long than the top. Bind them in place after trimming off the excess wire. Make sure they remain *on top* of each other. If they ride up on the side toward the top of the hook a bit, don't worry. I'll take care of that problem next if it should happen.

Step 22.3: Select a clump of feather fibers (I'm using hen back) and tie them to the end of the shank to form a tail no longer than the gape of the hook. Advance the thread to the front of the hook, then trim any waste fibers from the tail. Here I'm using my thumbnail to press them down on the top of the hook/wire strips to force them to the offside of the shank. I suggest applying a couple of drops of head cement or superglue to further anchor them in place. Let any glue dry before continuing.

Step 22.4: Place wax on the thread, and apply gray dubbing to it. Twist the dubbing into position on the thread, and wrap it over the hook to the end of the shank to form the body. (I want my thread clean of dubbing when I reach the end of the shank. With a little practice you will learn how much dubbing it takes to reach the back of the hook without having extra remaining.) Leave the bare thread hanging at the end of the shank.

Step 22.5: Wrap the bare thread forward over the body to form the rib. Once a tier "gets the feel" for the amount of dubbing required to cover the shank, making the body/rib is an incredibly fast process.

Step 22.6: Strip a small clump of fibers from the hen back feather, and tie them to the bottom of the hook to form a beard-style hackle. I like to fold the waste ends over and anchor them with the beard to make the unit more durable. Take care when trimming the waste to avoid cutting off the hackle. A whip-finish and a drop of head cement will complete the fly. (I've found on flies size 16 and smaller that one strand of lead wire on the offside of the hook is all that's required to give the fly the action needed to create the "illusion of life" the fish find so attractive.)

Chapter 23

Ostrich Herl Twist Nymph

This is a fly that Gary designed after we had scripted and filmed all of his patterns. Consequently, it was never on any of the videos or in print. Gary called Paul with the design of this fly, hoping that at some future time we could film it. Unfortunately that never happened. Gary's death brought his family, the four of us, and the fly-fishing world to a sudden stop. He left a void in all of our lives that's still felt today, years later.

Toward the end of his journey on this earth, Gary felt it was time to liquidate his fishing equipment. His daughter Heather and son-in-law Patrick helped him list the various items for sale on eBay and several other locations. Paul had the good fortune to purchase many of the items, including Gary's favorite "small stream rod"—a Sage 279 LLB 2-weight, 7-foot, 9-inch Graphite III.

When Paul purchased the rod, Gary sent a special letter to him telling about the rod and a snippet of his history with it taken from one of his journals. That letter along with a "moment in time" from his log book are the introduction to this chapter—the one fly never published and until today the information about his favorite rod never before seen by the public. It was one of the last items written by a fly-fishing legend. He wrote:

> For me this wonderful little 2-weight represented a philosophical statement. This was custom made for me from a Sage blank by Steve Oristian (a good fly-fishing friend from Maryland). It's a rod that I used a lot, but it was never a toy. It was always a practical fly-fishing tool.
>
> For me a toy is when someone takes a 2-weight out to a large river or lake where there are big trout. That person can hook big trout on a 2-weight, but it takes too long to land those fish on such a small rod. In that situation the rod is a dangerous toy. That's not where I used the Sage 279LLB. ... For me this was a small stream fly rod. I kept it strung up in my car on rod racks attached to the roof. Every small stream I crossed, I jumped out, grabbed this rod, and started casting with a dry fly or small nymph. Usually the trout were under 12 inches, but occasionally there was the brute that went up to 14 or 15 or 16 inches. There are always surprises in these small streams.

The 2-weight can handle a 16-inch fish quickly and efficiently. What it can't handle is a four or five pound trout out of the Henry's Fork or the Missouri. In the big river the large fish has too much room to run—and the small rod ends up killing them by playing them to death.

I'm going to include one listing from my fishing log for this fly rod—it's a typical 'small stream' day. September 15th—'...fishing Baggs Creek, a small tributary of Cottonwood Creek right near Deer Lodge. Baggs is a 10-minute drive from my home. I unloaded Chester and Zeb, and then pulled the 279 LLB off the upper rack. It was already strung up, and it already had a #16 Orange Double Wing tied on a 4x tippet. This seemed perfect because the leaves were already changing color along the stream.

'This is a great little brookie stream, with deep little holes and fine little runs. This one you can jump across in most spots. I walked straight up-stream, casting the dry fly into every little likely spot. Those brookies were ravenous. At 7'9" the 2-weight was perfect, keeping my loop under the can-opy of branches over my head. Chester behaved himself—Zeb didn't. We played keep-away with every trout with him. Most of the fish were between 6 and 11 inches, but one was 13 inches and in fall spawning colors. By the end of the day we had caught so many trout that even Zeb was tired—and he was starting to behave himself. He's learning to be a fishing dog. Chester is disgusted with him, though. He doesn't think we should bring the big dummy.'

I have had so many great days with this 279 LLB. It has been my small stream workhorse.

Paul is lucky to have this beautiful piece of memorabilia. He doesn't take it fishing, but I wish just once he'd take it to his special spring creek and use it one more time for Gary. You know the location, Paul—up near the place where the water bubbles out of the ground. The fish aren't too big, Paul. How about it? Take it out one more time. I think Gary would approve.

Ostrich Herl Twist Nymph

Hook: Size 10 to 20, 1x long nymph

Thread: Gray or color to match the body

Tail: Two ostrich herls

Abdomen: Gray ostrich herl and Antron touch dubbing, Double Magic style

Touch dubbing: Orange, yellow, pink, or color of choice

Wing case: Optional, gray Antron yarn strand or color of choice

Thorax: Gray ostrich herl

Head: Thread

Sometimes I add a wing case of Antron yarn, color to match the body. The original fly didn't have a wing case, so we'll follow that recipe here; but you may want to try a wing case at some future time.

Step 23.1: Place the hook in the vise, and lay down a thread base that covers the back half of the hook. Trim off the piece of waste thread. Be certain that piece of thread is at least 4 inches long. Set it aside for use in the next step.

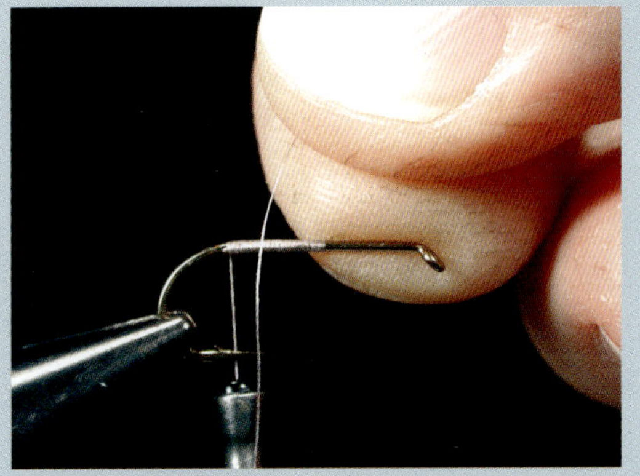

Step 23.2: Select two (gray) ostrich herl tips, and tie them to the back of the hook to use as a tail. Take the tag of waste thread left from the last step, pass it through the gape, pull it to the rear of the shank, and then over the hook, splitting the tails in the process as illustrated. Anchor the double thread strands to the hook shank; adjusting their tension determines how wide the tails are divided. Trim off the waste part of the "tail divider" to finish this step.

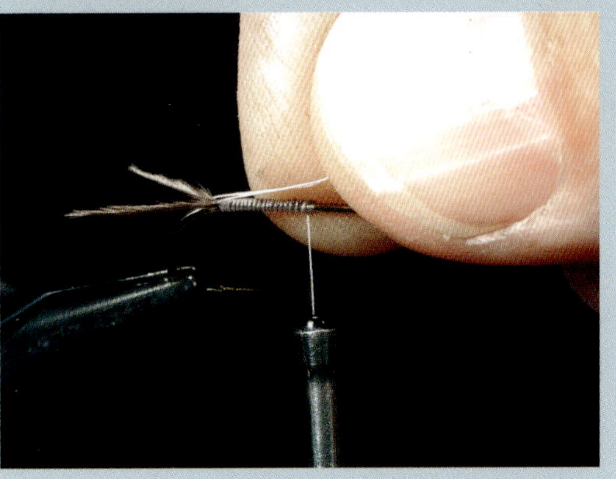

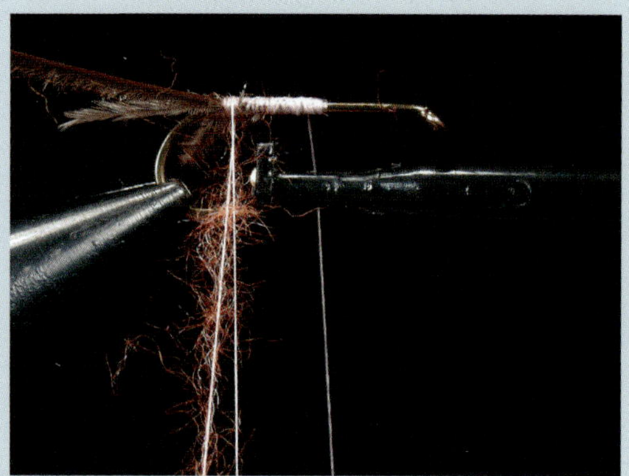

Step 23.3: Tie one ostrich herl to the back of the hook. Form the thread into a dubbing loop, and apply Super Tacky Wax to one side of it. Pat that side with orange touch dubbing. I like to use a long electronics test clip as a dubbing loop tool, but use what you have; they all work just fine.

Step 23.4: Secure the ostrich herl and the dubbing loop in the tool. Twist the tool to form ostrich herl chenille with orange Antron highlights. Wrap the chenille forward to the center of the hook, forming the abdomen.

Step 23.5: Trim off the excess herl and dubbing loop. Attach several (I used four) ostrich herls to the center of the hook while advancing the thread to the eye. Wrap the herls forward to form the thorax, then tie them off and trim the surplus. Gary tied the herls to the hook by their butt ends, and quite frankly I can't get the fly to look worth a darn unless I tie them to the shank by their tip ends. Use the method that works best for you.

Step 23.6: Apply a whip-finish, and trim the thread from the hook. Place a drop of head cement to complete the fly.

Chapter 24

Pheasant Tail Twist Nymph

OK, readers. I'm looking around the room (these pages) and have to ask this question: "How many of you use a Pheasant Tail Nymph? A bead-head version? How about a flash back?" I see by the show of [imaginary] hands that many of you have at least a few in your fly boxes if trout are your main quarry.

I have to admit that the Pheasant Tail Nymph in its many configurations used to be one of my top six flies. Notice the words "used to be" in the last sentence? What do you think might have happened to make me change my mind? If you guessed, "Gary LaFontaine," you'd be right.

I didn't really realize how much he had affected the way Gretchen and I approach our fishing until we were about halfway through this book. Gretchen was the one who really brought it to my attention. She was editing one of the chapters as I drove north out of Boise toward our weekend place on the Payette River. She asked me, "Is your 5-weight rod rigged with a fly and leader?" "Yeah," I responded. "What pattern do you have on the tippet?" "I don't know, I suppose a Lime Double Wing with a PT Twist dropper," I answered after a bit of thought, remembering the creek we had fished the previous weekend.

We drove in silence for a mile or so, both of us in deep thought; for me, Gary kept coming and going across my mind's eye. Gretchen jerked me back to the present day out of my daydream by asking, "What flies would you have had on your leader when you were guiding in Montana?" "I don't know, probably a Humpy or Royal Wulff with a bead-head something or other on a dropper." "When was the last time you fished a Humpy?" she asked a few minutes later. She had me there. I couldn't remember the last time I used that pattern, and it used to be in my top group of flies like its partner, the Pheasant Tail Nymph.

She didn't get the chapter edited like she had planned during our two-hour drive north. Instead we spent the last miles reviewing how our close association with Gary LaFontaine as well as Paul and Char Stimpson had changed our fishing and tying. I wouldn't go so far as to call it a "life altering" experience, but darned near it!

We compared imaginary fly boxes in years past with those we had in our vests today. Yes, all the old favorites were somewhere in our vests or wader bags;

we just couldn't remember where. My favorite fly of all time had been a standard Renegade; today it is the Enchanted Renegade, following Paul's lead when he used Gary's Double Magic body style on a Prince Nymph. I had stolen the idea and applied it to many of my favorites, including the Renegade. In some cases Gary's pattern had completely replaced an old favorite like the fly in this chapter, the Pheasant Tail Twist Nymph; I wasn't sure if I had any regular PT Nymphs in my fly boxes or not. (I just spent the last half hour looking through my wader bag and vest before returning to the keyboard. I finally did find a few PTs in the bottom of the wet bag I carry in my wader bag with a change of clothes in case I fall in the water—which happens more than I'd like to admit.)

As I slowed down for the "reduced speed" zone in Cascade, I commented with a grin, "It sure is too bad that Gary screwed up our fishing so bad!" "Yeah," Gretchen responded, "and now we catch so darned many more fish it ought to be illegal! I wonder why?"

All of you reading this book are probably sick of listening to me tell you about "another great pattern," so I'll let you make your own conclusion regarding this fly. Just don't ask to borrow a PT Nymph. I took the box of them out of my wet bag a few minutes ago and left them in the garage. I won't be needing them! I have plenty of another pattern to imitate my Baetis or Callibaetis nymphs.

Pheasant Tail Twist Nymph

Hook: Size 8 to 22, 1x nymph

Thread: Brown

Tail: Two pheasant tail fibers, divided

Abdomen: One pheasant tail fiber, orange touch dubbing

Wing case: Several pheasant tail fibers

Thorax: Olive touch dubbing

Head: Thread

Like its cousin the PT Nymph, I think this fly is great when tied as a bead head, a flash back, or with a Double Magic peacock herl thorax. Just let your imagination be your guide.

Step 24.1: Start the thread in the center of the hook, and wrap back to the end of the shank. *Do not* trim off the tag of thread; we'll use it in the next function.

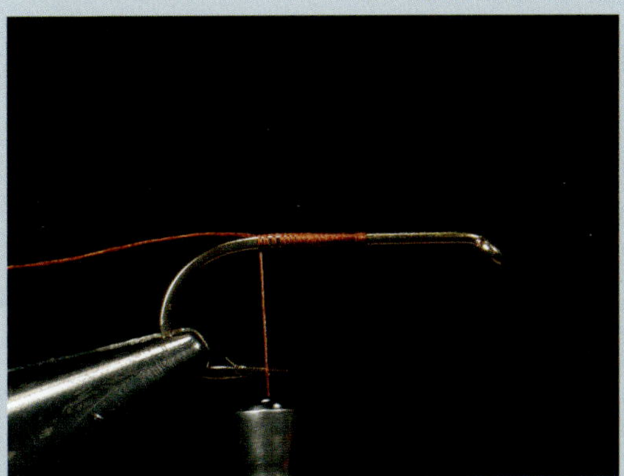

Step 24.2: Strip two pheasant tail fibers from the stem, tie them to the back of the shank to start a tail that is as long as the gape of the hook, and trim off the waste. Pull the extra tag of thread from the previous step between the two fibers to keep them separated. Anchoring the thread to the shank completes the tail. (In the last chapter I illustrated a similar method of dividing the tail. This is just another way to accomplish the same task. You'll find it used throughout these pages.)

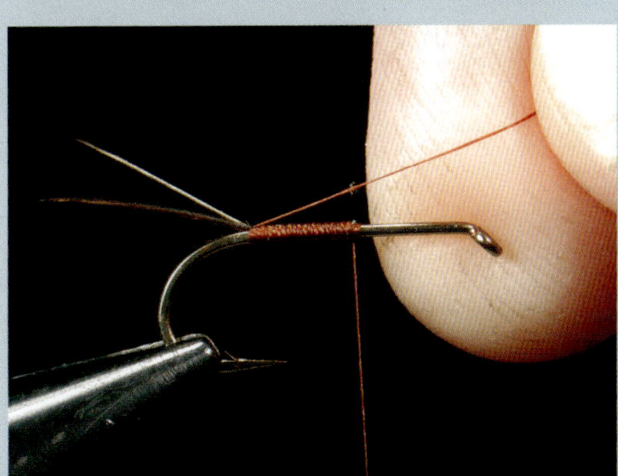

Step 24.3: Trim off the waste end of the thread. Strip a couple of pheasant tail fibers (use only one on size 14 and smaller), and tie them to the back of the shank. Trim off the waste ends, and leave the thread hanging at the back of the hook.

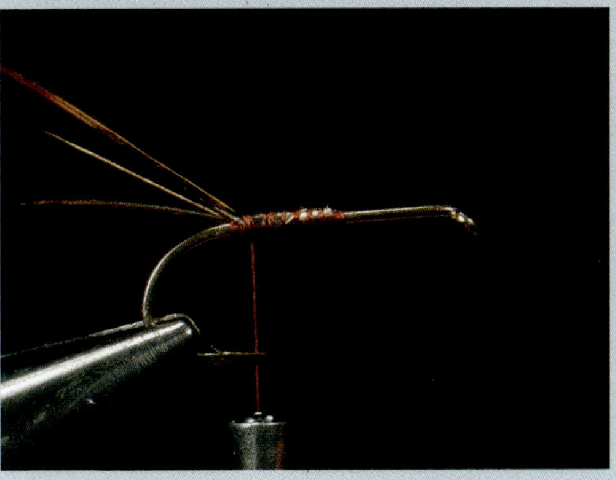

Step 24.4: Apply Super Tacky Wax to the thread, then pat it with a clump of orange touch dubbing. Form the thread into a dubbing loop, capturing it *and* the pheasant tail fibers with a dubbing-loop tool. Twist the thread and the pheasant tail fibers together, then wrap them over the back part of the hook to form the Antron-highlighted abdomen. Tie off the materials, and trim them from the hook.

Step 24.5: Pull several pheasant tail fibers from the feather, and tie them to the center of the hook with the tips pointing to the rear. Stroke the thread with wax, and pat it with medium-olive touch dubbing. *Do not* twist the dubbing around the thread; instead just wrap it forward to form the thorax. I like to stroke back the dubbing after each turn of the thread, but that is a personal preference; apply your dubbing as you wish.

Step 24.6: Pull over the pheasant tail fibers to form a wing case. Anchor them at the front of the hook, and clip off the waste ends. Rather than cutting off the waste ends, they can be pulled back into legs if you feel they are an important part of your fly. I often do so, but today we are following Gary's recipe, not mine. Whip-finish, trim the thread, and apply head cement to complete the fly.

Chapter 25

Roll Over Mysis Shrimp

When we left Denver, a cold September wind was blowing and there was a threat of snow in the high mountains along Highway 70. Thankfully we got over the pass without a mishap and eventually turned off the freeway toward our home in Delta at Grand Junction. We stopped briefly at the mouth of Escalante Canyon to let Dubbin (our fishing dog) go for a run while Gretchen let me know we could soon expect company.

On the last day of the show she had run into Alberto Salvini and Marika Cicoria (fly-fishing friends from Rome, Italy), and they had asked her if it would be OK if they visited for a couple of days sometime during the next week or so. She had told them to stop in any time. Almost as an afterthought, she added their special request: "Oh, by the way, they need some big fish pictures for a magazine article because their San Juan River trip didn't produced what they needed." We were under the gun, so to speak, to find good fishing on short notice. We'd have to think about that for a time.

We arrived home, unloaded the truck, and headed for the office—me to download messages from the answering machine and Gretchen to review several days' worth of mail the neighbor had collected for us. The last message on the machine was from Marika, advising us that they planned to arrive the next day *and* she was going to fix us an authentic Italian dinner. That sure made me smile. On the positive side, a dinner prepared by a beautiful, blonde Italian lady sounded great. The negative part of the equation was that we needed to find a "big fish place" in short order.

The Taylor River was just such a place, but it had one little problem: We had fished there four or five times and never could catch one of the big fish that lived there. When we talk about big fish, I really mean "huge" fish, but they didn't reach their large size by being stupid. At least for us, they had proven to be really difficult (impossible) to catch. Thankfully we had recently returned from a visit with Gary, and one of the patterns we had discussed was the Roll Over Mysis Shrimp. I had tied several samples after returning home and put them in my fishing vest, where they sat in limbo waiting for their opportunity.

Late the next afternoon Alberto and Marika arrived for their visit. While Gretchen and Marika prepared an authentic Italian dinner (I could hardly wait), Alberto and I discussed "options" for the next couple of days' fishing. When I mentioned the big fish at the Taylor River, he said it was the place he wanted to investigate. When I cautioned that the fish were really difficult to catch, he said, "I can catch anything!" We had fished with our Italian friends several times in past years, and I had to believe him. Alberto is a "fly-fishing vacuum cleaner"; he is that good.

The plan was set; we would go there the next day. We arrived at the river early the next morning, but not soon enough to beat the crowd of people who were there hoping to catch one of the big fish. Gretchen grabbed her rod (with no fly on it) and eased into a spot on the bank, pretending to fish while Alberto rigged up his rod. Marika (the photographer) set up her Nikon and joined Gretchen on the bank. We had to wait until several people gave up on the large fish in frustration and left. I grabbed my rod (also without a fly) and took up my beat on the bank next to Gretchen, leaving room for Alberto to slip in between us. Our job was to give him plenty of space to get a chance to catch some fish so that Marika could capture the moment.

A half hour later, Alberto finally hooked a fish, but it was not one of the big boys; it was only 21 inches. He landed it, and Marika shot the photograph. Back at the water's edge we heard a yip of surprise. We turned around to see that Dubbin had taken a seat on a large rock right where the river made a turn downstream on its trip to join the Gunnison at Almont. He had waited for a couple of anglers to leave before claiming his vantage point. Good dog! He has manners!

A couple of minutes later a trout jumped out of the water, clearing the surface almost 3 feet and not much more than a foot in front of Dubbin's nose. We heard another yip, but this time we saw the fish. After seeing the fish, Alberto had to give it a try; he spent the better part of three hours trying everything in his bag of tricks to bring that fish to hand, but no luck. Dubbin stayed "glued" to that rock the whole afternoon, yipping every time that fish cleared the water. That happened about every five minutes all the time we were there. We never did figure out what it was feeding on.

After admitting the trout was "difficult," Alberto dropped back downstream next to us (we were still running "crowd control") and caught several more smaller fish between 18 and 22 inches. We had had enough and told our friends we would see them at home whenever they got there. As an afterthought, I gave Alberto three of Gary's Roll Over Mysis Shrimp patterns I had tied earlier, telling him how Gary suggested they be offered to the fish. We headed for home.

About midnight our friends arrived back at the house, and they were excited. We had fallen asleep in front of the television, so there was no way we could escape to bed without hearing the story.

At "dark thirty" the big fish had left its post in the faster current and moved into the quieter pool below the big rock. Alberto had cast Gary's pattern to it, letting it hang upside-down in the quiet water. Just as the fish swam over to take a look at the fly, Alberto tugged ever so slightly on his line, causing the fly to flip over. The fish ate it, and the fight was on. Marika finally did get a picture of the fish as Alberto eased it into the shallows to land it, but the camera flash spooked the big fish; it took off, snapping the leader in the process. They estimated the fish was over 30 inches, but they never got it close enough to get a hand on it. We didn't have to worry about entertaining them for the next couple of days; they spent all of their time on the Taylor River but never did trick old big boy again.

The next day, after Alberto and Marika headed back to the Taylor River, Gretchen asked me, "Have you noticed something wrong with Dubbin?" I had noticed him acting "funny," but in the turmoil of getting our friends off on the day's excursion, I hadn't paid any attention to him. Upon closer inspection, we saw that his face was badly swollen and his normally dark-brown nose had a definite red color to it. We loaded him in the car and took him to the vet. Eighty dollars later we learned that a dog could get sunburn on his nose if he watches fish in the river too long on a hot, sunny day! You just never know when you'll find a new thing to learn. Did you know a dog could get sunburn? We didn't then, but we sure do now and apply a band of sunscreen across the top of his nose on every outing. No more trips to the vet for Dubbin—at least not for that reason.

Roll Over Mysis Shrimp

Hook: Size 10 to 16, 3x long curved nymph

Thread: White

Rib: White thread

Weight: Lead wire strip (nonlead substitute)

Tail: White hackle fibers

Body: White marabou

Eye: Melted monofilament

Head: White marabou dubbing

When I asked Gary why he used a loop to form the body on this pattern rather than dubbing the marabou directly on the hook in the normal fashion (a much easier process), he answered that the field team had tested both and found that the fish seemed to like the clipped version better.

Gray materials were used in the illustrations rather than white as suggested in the recipe to help provide photographic clarity.

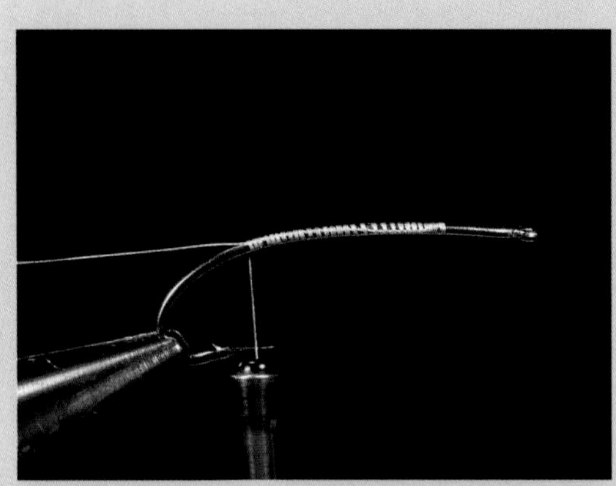

Step 25.1: Mount the hook in the vise; wrap a thread base that starts at the one-fourth position and stops at the end of the shank (directly above the hook barb). Be sure to leave a long tag of waste thread. That's not waste; it will be the rib in a future step. Store it in a material spring to use later.

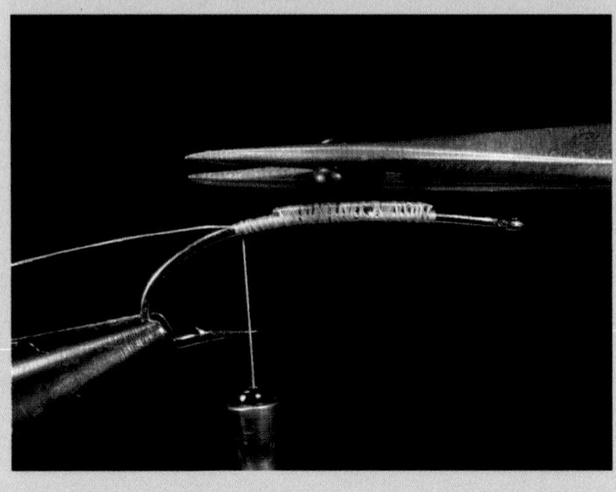

Step 25.2: Tie a strand of lead (or nonlead) wire to the *top* of the hook that is long enough to almost reach the end of the shank. Trim off waste. Cut a 2-inch section of monofilament, place it in a set of Sure Grip tweezers, and melt a set of eyes. Set the tweezers and eyes down to cool on the tabletop in the position I'm holding them in the illustration. This will allow them to cool/set without contacting the table's surface. I've found the absolute best monofilament for melting eyes is the strands in a truck or motor-home mudguard; they melt evenly and are always black.)

Step 25.3: Line up the tips of several white hackle fibers, and tie them to the hook to form a tail equal in length to the gape. Bind the waste ends over the lead strip remaining from the last step. Leave the bobbin hanging at the back of the hook.

Step 25.4: Form a dubbing loop, wrap the thread forward to the front of the hook, and apply Tacky Wax to one side of it (the loop). Clip the real fuzzy fibers from the base of a marabou feather, and slip them into the loop; the wax on one side helps hold the fibers in place. Attach a dubbing twister tool (I'm using an electronics test clip) to the loop, and twist the thread/material into fuzzy, marabou chenille. Wrap the chenille forward to meet the thread, stroking back the fibers after each turn. Tie off the chenille, and trim the excess from the hook.

Step 25.5: At this point the unfinished fly is (at best) a wild mess. Therefore, I like to whip-finish the thread and trim it from the hook temporarily while I shape the body with a pair of scissors. Trim the body to shape, then tie the thread back on the hook and trim the tag end.

Step 25.6: Counterwrap the rib over the body, and anchor it at the front of the hook. Clip the rib material from the hook.

Step 25.7: Set the melted eyes in place on the shank, and anchor them with several crisscross wraps. The Sure Grip tweezers make holding the eyes in position to attach them to the hook a very easy process. If I try to use my fingers, I often drop the eyes before getting them on the hook.

Step 25.8: Apply wax to the thread, then dub (and twist) a small clump of marabou fibers to it. Wrap a dubbed marabou head.

Step 25.9: A half-hitch tool makes tying off the thread on this pattern a lot easier. Clip the thread from the hook, and add a drop of head cement to complete the fly.

Chapter 26

Variegated Midge Larva

"Hey, Al, what's this?" Gretchen called to me this last weekend at our home away from home on the river. I was having trouble getting the Weed Whacker started and was more than happy to take a much-needed break. *Have you ever noticed what a miserable piece of equipment a gas engine can be when it decides it doesn't want to start?* I pondered as I wandered over to the gazebo by the water to see what the topic of her question could be.

"Look at this," she prompted as I walked up, "It's the biggest midge I've ever seen." There on the gazebo screen was a gray-body adult midge that had to be at least a size 10, maybe even an 8. The morning dew and chill in the air had it anchored to the screen, giving us ample time to study it.

Further investigation brought a plethora of aquatic insects into our view on the screen, waiting for the warming morning air to allow them to escape. In the meantime we could study them at our leisure; and study them we certainly did. *It's amazing what a grown man will do to get out of work,* I thought, glancing at the recalcitrant string trimmer, then focusing my attention back on the insects "resting" on the screen.

Without really realizing it, we had stumbled onto a bird's-eye view of the bugs available to the trout in the river. It was like using a seine in the current, but we didn't have to put on waders and enter the water to study the biomass. It was right in front of us, so we could see everything up close and personal. I grabbed the magnifying glass out of my DeLorme map of Idaho so that I could look at the insects a bit closer.

I had never taken the time to see them in such detail before, and the experience was really interesting. There were many more large midges than I had ever realized might be in our stretch of river. I asked Gretchen (and myself as well), "Should we have been using some larger midge patterns last night when we tried our luck on the river?" I didn't get an answer as I heard a door close nearby. *She must have heard the phone ringing,* I said to myself as I went back to my "weed-eating" project.

This time the contrary machine started, and an hour later I had the grass along the bank trimmed. I went looking for Gretchen to make good on my promise to take her into town for a late breakfast before the kids arrived for a barbecue that afternoon. I found her at the vise cranking out flies—large midge patterns, to be exact. "The kids called to say they couldn't make it this afternoon but would see us in the morning," she advised as I sat down at my vise next to hers. "We've got a free afternoon, and I think we should go fishing," she stated emphatically. Darned, I hate it when she's right; but who was I to argue?

I looked at the flies she was tying and commented that she must have been looking at the outline for this book. The next chapter was Gary's Variegated Midge Larva, and she had several of them lying in front of her, with one minor difference. Hers were all large (size 10 and 12) instead of the traditional smaller size. Wow! What a great idea.

We put the flies in our vests and in no time were into our waders headed downriver to a favorite spot; somehow breakfast was forgotten in the process. A few minutes later we arrived at the place where underwater structure produced a great feeding lane; the trout were already gobbling something in the surface film. The oversize flies were Gretchen's idea, so I gave her first shot at the fish while Dubbin and I sat down on the bank to observe. The second cast brought an average-size fish to the bank—a 13-inch rainbow, nothing special but a lot of fun. I told her to keep on fishing; I was enjoying watching her and would take my turn in due course.

Several casts later she hung a better-than-average fish that took off like it was shot out of a gun. It headed to the middle of the river and wrapped the leader around a sunken log. That was the end of that. She was muttering to herself as she climbed the bank and sat down next to the dog and me. "I should have had that fish," she groused. Being a smart husband, I kept quiet. "It's your turn," she said and started tying another length of tippet to her broken leader.

I walked a short distance up the bank, then dropped into the water so that I could make a downstream-and-across presentation to the other side of a rock I had been studying. I had tied a Variegated Midge Larva on a dropper under a Lime Double Wing so that my poor eyes could get an idea of what was happening beyond the end of my rod. My first cast landed just where I wanted it and had drifted about 3 feet when the Double Wing disappeared in a swirl. I was into another better-than-average-fish, but it didn't run straight for the middle of the river like Gretchen's had. It stayed deep by the rock, shook its head, and sulked, but I couldn't move it. Finally it just turned, flipping its tail in the air (that looked to me to be as wide as my hand) and slowly swam downstream. It didn't pick up speed; it didn't pay any attention to the pressure I placed on it through my fly rod. It just got into its car, closed the door, and drove away. When I had two turns of backing left on my reel. I dropped the rod tip and broke it off.

Gretchen and I just looked at each other, stunned. We had fished this stretch of river almost every weekend during the summer for the past three years, and our biggest fish had been around 15 inches. What happened last weekend is a mystery to us both, except this time we were fishing Gretchen's oversize Variegated Midge Larva. Was this fly the difference, or did we just happen onto some larger fish that had moved in from parts unknown? We don't know and have to leave this chapter (and the book) with a mystery for which we have no answer. If any of you come up with answers of your own, please let us know. It would be fun to learn about your experiences. Now don't blink, because this fly is so easy to tie you could easily miss it if you're not careful!

Variegated Midge Larva

Hook: Size 14 to 22 (or maybe bigger), 1x long wet fly
Thread: Olive
Body: Red and olive marabou, one strand of each
Body accent: Clear Antron, one strand
Spike: White Antron, extending over the eye

Gray materials were used in the illustrations rather than white as suggested in the recipe to help provide photographic clarity.

Step 26.1: Set the hook in the vise, and attach the thread to the shank directly behind the eye. Wrap to the end of the shank, and trim off the waste piece of thread.

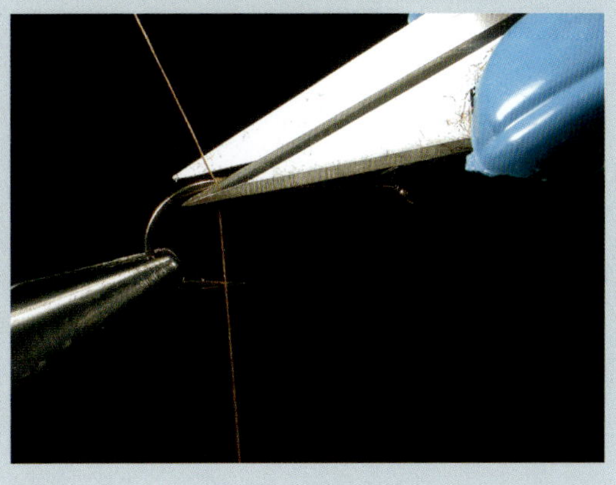

Step 26.2: Select one strand each of red and olive marabou, and tie them to the end of the shank by their butt ends. Take one strand of clear Antron, and tie it on top of the marabou. If you are tying some of Gretchen's oversize patterns, then use two or three strands of each material. Leave the bobbin hanging at the front of the hook.

Step 26.3: Secure the three materials in a hackle pliers or an electronics test clip. Twist the tool to form a rope-type material from the marabou and Antron. Wrap it forward to meet the thread at the front of the hook. Tie it off, and trim the waste end.

Step 26.4: Select a strand of white Antron, and tie it to the front of the hook to form a short spike. Trim off the surplus, leaving behind a short tag of material behind the spike.

Step 26.5: Take several turns of thread in front of the spike to tilt it up slightly. Whip-finish the thread, then trim it from the hook.

Step 26.6: Use a fine-tooth comb to fluff the fibers in the spike. The fly is ready to go fishing. (Don't forget to let us know how it works for you and to help us with the puzzle. Does a large Variegated Midge catch fish for you? Good fishing!)

It's kind of funny the way things work out. As these pages unfolded before Gretchen and me, there were times when they seemed to appear magically. However, there were other times we just could not get our thoughts from our brains into the computer. A flashing cursor is a very frustrating thing when it's alone on a blank screen.

Gretchen commented the other evening, as we drove north out of Boise toward a weekend on the river, "It seems like we were guided at times." I have to agree and would further her comment by saying that we would run into a "brick wall" if we weren't going in the right direction. "So, who was guiding you?" one might ask. Neither one of us knows for sure, but we have finally accepted the fact that our "perception of what Gary would want" was our guiding light. If in our hearts we were going in a direction Gary wouldn't have liked, then we seemed to block ourselves rather than produce something he would not have wanted.

Is this book what Gary LaFontaine would have written about his fly patterns? No, it's not. It's about his patterns of course, but it is how they (and their originator) affected us (your authors), not how he would have presented them himself. Only he could know how to accomplish that task, as he did so eloquently in past publications.

Gary had a way of pushing a person to excel without that person really understanding he or she was were being gently pushed to "reach for the sky." Let me give you just one of many examples.

We were more than halfway through the "video project" when I discovered he had gently nudged us toward his vision of a completed project. Of course we had input, but we were definitely guided to the end result. I hadn't really realized it until we were scripting one of the first marabou body flies. Gary suggested we cut the marabou off the stem, apply it to the hook using a dubbing loop, and then clip the body to shape. Paul and I disagreed with him, basing our position from a commercial tier's perspective. It took a heck of a lot longer to apply the marabou using the dubbing loop/trimming process than several other methods that produced similar-looking results. In all cases Gary backed away from his position until the field team had stream-tested any application methods in question, where the crew allowed the real critics (the trout) to make the final decision. After the trout spoke, the subject was closed. What's funny is that in most cases, the fish selected Gary's position. He just seemed to know what they would want—and unfortunately the trout never cared one bit what a couple of commercial tiers thought would be a faster method of producing the fly.

In time we learned to accept Gary's belief without questioning, but there were several "lively conversations" until we all reached that point. Unfortunately for me, I had a harder head than the others. It took me longer to "fall in line," but I did eventually get there. What I appreciated so much about him during this process is the good humor and smile that were part of the game.

That humor and smile spread into almost all aspects of the relationship the four of us shared with him. At times we would spend the better part of a day trying to get some work done, and Gary would keep all of us in stitches laughing. We all knew we were in trouble if he started a story with the statement, "Now this [story] is mostly true!" What would follow could be the most outlandish fabrication *or* a tale that really made a lot of sense, except it would be just bit "off." I'd think to myself, *That sounds like it could have happened*. But I would keep wondering when Gary would jerk the rug out from under me with the "punch line" as only he could deliver it. Sometimes it really was "mostly true"; we just never knew for certain which category he had skillfully laid out before us.

Take fly-fishing dogs as an example. Gary always believed his dog, Chester, was the best fishing dog in the world, while Gretchen and I disagreed. We really believed our companion, Dubbin, was the best fishing dog the world had to offer. Unfortunately we can't tell a story as well as Gary could. In fact we do not have a "Dubbin tale" to share with you; we just love fly fishing with him. Therefore, I guess, Chester has more credibility by default than Dubbin does. See what you think after reading the following "Chester story" from www.thebookmailer.com; thanks to Cathy and Marcie.

In Praise of Dogs—and Also Me

Gary LaFontaine

The world's most famous fly-fishing dog, my boy Chester, is about ten years old now, and he's fished at least a hundred days a year every day of his life. In countless photographs of me fishing, ones that have appeared in magazines and books, there's Chester right by my side. He has been on television shows with me, floating rivers, hiking up to mountain lakes, and wading the streams. He's the star in three best-selling fly-fishing videos, stealing the show from his two-legged angling buddies. Most people love Chester, however, because of the stories about him in my books. It's there that they get to know the true character of the World's Greatest Fly Fishing Dog.

Anyone who watches Chester "fish" ends up wide-eyed in amazement. It is hilarious, but Chester isn't trying to be funny. The humor is how ruthless, how relentless, how focused he is on the water. He can't actually "fish," so the human standing next to him has to do the fishing for him. And that human had better do it right.

Steve Oristian came to Montana to fish with me. A friend asked him if he was intimidated by the idea of fishing with a fly-fishing writer. This was the first time Steve was actually going to fish with me, but he quickly found out that I'm a very easygoing fellow on the stream. Steve had to fish with Chester, though—and he called up his friend and told him, "Chester is the one who is the tough one to fish with."

We were on the North Fork of the Blackfoot River, and I put Steve on a pool with wicked, mixed currents. He stood there with Chester right next to him, casting a dry fly to big cutthroats; but the tumbling water kept dragging his fly, and that made him miss the strikes of the slow, deliberate risers. Steve missed the first strike, and he gave an outraged yell. Then he glanced down and asked me, "Did Chester just give me a dirty look?"

"That's his fish."

Steve cast again and missed a second trout. Chester actually stepped back to look at him this time. Steve cast a third time, and when drag snatched the fly, he missed the third trout. Chester looked at him one more time, and then he stalked off the stream. Steve was muttering, "I can't believe it. I'm not good enough for him. He left me. A dog left me. Chester, come back."

For the rest of the week Steve fished magnificently, getting better every day, his skill levels pushed higher and higher by the dog standing by his side. And when he would net a fish, and hold it out for Chester to kiss, he would ask, "How am I doing, buddy?"

Chester actually helps me catch more fish—by my own tally, Chester adds more than a hundred trout a season to my total catch. Only a con- firmed dog-hater wouldn't want Chester with him on the water. My fishing friends want Chester with them on the water.

Jeff Pill called me up last summer: "Gary, I'll be coming through Montana next week. I'll be driving right through your town, and right down your street. I was wondering if Chester can go fishing?"

Usually my friends pick up Chester, but they let me come along, too. Sometimes when we go to familiar spots and I'm there with more than one person, I'll go with one angler and send Chester with the other. Chester can read water, leading the way up the stream for a fisherman. And he stops if a trout rises, staring at the spot where the fish rose on the river.

During the Callibaetis mayfly hatch on ponds near my home in Mon- tana, my faithful dog is my alarm clock. I've never been much of a morning person. Usually I stay up working until two or three in the morning, and then sleep until almost noon, but in August the Callibaetis start emerging at 9:30 a.m. That hatch is definitely at an inconvenient time.

During the summer months I keep working all night, and then at dawn I'll drive out to my favorite ponds. There are four of these ponds, known as the Job Corp Ponds, about 14 miles from my home in Deer Lodge. I'll park by either Pond #1 or Pond #3, string up my fly rod, inflate my Water

Master kick boat, and then with Chester riding on the back, paddle out onto the water. Everything is calm, the morning sun is just beginning to kill the night chill, and nothing is going to happen on the surface for at least four hours. I stretch out and go to sleep. Chester curls up in back, right by my head, and does the same thing. I'm such a sound sleeper that I would snore my way through a feeding frenzy by the biggest slob trout in the whole pond, but at 9:30 a.m., when the first fish rises to that first Callibaetis dun, Chester hears it and immediately stands up, starts circling around, steps on my head, and wakes me up. I know that it's time to start fishing, and to find trout I follow Chester's eyes.

That's just one way he helps me catch fish.

Jeff produced the videos *Successful Fly Fishing Strategies,* pairing up Dick Sharon and me for the on-camera fishing, but he also put Chester into a starring role. There were two clowns and a straight man—and the straight man was a dog. When we started filming, one of the production people warned us that an untrained dog in the shoot would be a disaster. We just laughed at him. There was nothing untrained about Chester when he was fishing. Nothing could be more predictable. He was an angler, standing right by my side, his eyes on the fly or the strike indicator, fishing out every cast. He knew how to spot, stalk, and watch the playing and release of trout. Chester was such a great addition to the action that Jack Dennis even flew him down with us in a private plane to fish the Green River, the section below Flaming Gorge Reservoir in Utah. We filmed the video *Tying and Fishing Attractors* there.

The ancient Teutons, the ancestors of the Germans, had a saying: "All good dogs go to heaven." Chester, my German Shepherd mongrel, is a very good dog, but heaven had better have trout streams or Chester isn't going. Chester is a fishing dog, instinctively born to fish just like some dogs are born to hunt birds. I didn't purposely choose him as a pup for this—my daughter snatched him up from the side of the road when he fell out of the back of a truck. The truck kept going, the handful of puppy was frightened but unharmed, and I had eight pounds of new dog.

I couldn't have picked a more perfect fly-fishing dog. There are good dogs for fishing, and there are bad dogs for fishing. Believe it or not, I know what it is like to fish with a few bad dogs. Still, no one loves to fish with dogs more than I do. Great fishing dogs, good fishing dogs, poor fishing dogs, even horrible fishing dogs—I love to be on the water with them all.

Whether this story is mostly true or not, I couldn't agree more with Gary. Gretchen and my most wonderful times together are those we spend with Dubbin in the driftboat on the Yellowstone River. Whether Chester or Dubbin is the perfect fly-fishing dog will not be settled within these pages; I'm not even sure history will provide that answer. But who cares? Let's go fishing!

Learn Fly Tying from The Experts!

Fly Tyer®

THE WORLD'S ONLY MAGAZINE Dedicated to the Art of Fly Tying.

Every quarterly issue is packed with superb, step-by-step photographs and precise instructions for tying the most innovative patterns for all varieties of game fish. Whether you're a newcomer to the sport or a veteran angler looking for an edge, you will find everything you need to improve your skills at the fly-tying vise.

Classic Patterns
Perfect your tying techniques on dry flies, nymphs and terrestrials.

Hot New Flies
Be the first to tie and cast fly fishing's most innovative patterns.

Bass Buggin'
Discover the tying tricks that will help you catch more bass and panfish.

Saltwater Basics
Tie flies worthy of the planet's largest and most powerful game fish.

Tyer Profiles
Our master anglers will show you how to increase your tying skills.

Tools & Materials
Learn what's new on the fly-shop shelves.

Don't Miss a Step. Subscribe Now!

Subscribe today by calling 1-800-397-8159

4 issues (1 Year) at $19⁹⁵

When calling, please mention code N7BFTM

Fly Tyer is published quarterly. Regular cover price is $5.99. In Canada add $10 per year. All other foreign add $20 per year. All payments in U.S. funds. Please allow 6 to 8 weeks for delivery of the first issue.